My B _g_

Graham Forrester

To Mary my wife, without whom this trip would have been intolerable and certainly not possible......... oh and a hairy caterpillar.

Cycling releases a chemical that makes you feel smug and superior all day.

Mark Steel (comedian and cyclist)

Yellow wakes me up in the morning
Yellow gets me on the bike every day
Yellow has taught me the meaning of sacrifice
Yellow makes me suffer
Yellow is the reason I'm here

Lance Armstrong (enough said)

Introduction

The invention of the modern bicycle, at least the most popular and commercially successful one, was in the 1860s and is accredited to father and son Pierre and Ernest Michaux of France, very apt since the most famous cycle race of all is held in that country over 3 weeks every July, le bicyclette was born. Katie Melua, the Georgian-English singer also sang about there being nine million of them in Bejing in her haunting song of 2007, now I don't know whether that's true or not but according to the statistics of the day there were 450 million bikes in the whole of China, 20 million in the UK alone with over a billion around the world, quite unbelievable.

These are a few facts about the ubiquitous machine, the bicycle, which of course has 2 wheels but there are tricycles having 3 wheels and unicycles 1 wheel, the latter being for the most extreme people amongst us. If I was to take a wild guess I would say that probably 99% of the population of England has ridden a cycle at some time in their life.

Even Mark Twain advocated learning to ride a bicycle and I'm sure that other American, the Texan Lance Armstrong would agree with his sentiment, for he is credited with saying; "Learn to ride a bicycle. You will not regret it if you live". Thankfully I did live and have certainly not regretted it. I started to cycle at an early age as a toddler on 3 wheels, a most robust trike with a luggage compartment between the back two wheels but as to the colour and make my memory has failed me.

As the years went by I passed the tri-cycling stage and moved onto my first two wheeler, a definite rite of passage, it was a Raleigh, red with white mudguards and a bigger bell than the Flying squad from Dixon of Dock Green, beautiful. It was bought for my birthday and after the usual training by my dad 'one push and off you go' I eventually managed the balancing act and up and down the street I went with my friends. Later we ventured further afield, only the adjoining streets mind you, as the years rolled on.

In the area were I lived all the streets were interconnected so that in our naivety we thought you could cycle to Liverpool and Manchester without even going on a main road, still thinking about it now with a bit of planning it probably would have been possible. Even so in those days of the late fifties, it seemed as though you could slalom around the cat's eyes in the middle of the road there was that little traffic to contend with, unlike now where cycle lanes are deemed a necessity by the authorities they are throughout large towns and cities.

I suppose I could look back through rose coloured glasses of that far gone era and say I could have been the next Milk Race (now called the Tour of Britain) winner but to be honest I was never the best rider or the strongest of the bunch even though I was one of the older boys. The art of riding without hands, a must to be in with the crowd in my day, also eluded me for far longer than my peers, who could even perform that trick with their hands in their pockets in winter and ride as quickly as I could with a four point hold!

Eventually I outgrew my red bike and badgered my mum and dad for a replacement, finally I got one, unfortunately it was not new but an old one which had been recycled from my mum. A black sit up and beg Elswick, not thankfully, with a basket but with iron brakes and iron everything else including the weighty Sturmy Archer three gear attached to the back wheel, oh and minus a crossbar naturally. It weighed an absolute 'ton' street cred would have definitely taken a nose dive, would I have ever recovered? Obviously not, so other plans had to be made. I walked.

Later at the tender age of 16 or thereabouts I found a bike frame, a 50's Sun Manxman no less, dumped on some waste ground. It had a bottom bracket and a headset but very little else that was usable but it was as though I'd found some buried treasure, my very own bike. It was blue with chrome front and rear forks which by now had become unchromed steel in need of a lot of tlc and a lot of tlc it got.

I managed over a period of time to beg steal and borrow bits for the bike until it was ride-able. I only had one brake so a fixed wheel was needed; a cog of 12 teeth was all I could get. Alright I know that they are sprockets not cogs the purists will tell me but in our vernacular of the day they were cogs just as wickets were timber and a football field was the park. However, the gearing was so high it was really difficult to start but a dream once you got going except when you went downhill and your legs were nearly rotated off your body!

At this particular time the famous Jacques Anquetil was the man of the moment achieving wonders in the Tour de France, a consecutive winner four times no less with five overall.

Our hero though of course was our own Tommy, the great Tom Simpson, winner of the UCI World Championship Road Race in San Sebastián in 1965, Anquetil could only make second a year later. I know I know Beryl Burton was around as a role model but she was a 'girl' after all, although I do earnestly agree she was a marvellous cyclist but unfortunately she like Tommy died before her time, 58 in her case, with heart failure during a training ride, dangerous stuff this cycling!

Around the roads we travelled on our bikes emulating our heroes of the cycling world and me doing a great impression of Tommy on Ventoux in 1967 (me dying metaphorically) every time I came to a big hill with my 12s cog. I personally never joined a cycling club, couldn't be bothered really but one of our group did, the Wigan Wheelers as I recall. I don't think he took it too seriously either, since my abiding memory of him was riding off to town dressed for the 'Tour' with a fag hanging out of his mouth!

Good days they were though and the sun always seemed to shine as we set off on our adventures with our home made butty bags strapped over our shoulders and cycling shoes clipped onto our pedals.

I remember going to Southport about 20 miles away with a friend of mine and two girls in tow neither of which could cycle very well. On the way we had to go up and over a local hill, the going down being a 17% gradient. Of course we two shot down, as boys will, leaving the ladies trailing, only to be stopped by a police car for exceeding the speed limit, 70 miles an hour they said, now in later life I realised they were joking but at the time did my chest puff out.

After the altercation with the Bobbies we waited for the girls but of them there was no sign, so back up we went, remember 17%, to find near the top, one of them had fallen off and landed on her nose, blood everywhere, the ambulance had already been called so, end of the ride. I'm glad to say she recovered well and we remained friends, until she looked into a mirror!

Throughout my later teens I was bequeathed my brother's bike when the pubs came a calling, for he was a few years older than me, funnily enough his bike was also a Sun Manxman but much better than mine with all the necessary bits intact and gears, four only but a luxury. My old bike did full circle and ended up back on a tip with the fondest of memories and more than a tinge of regret. I continued riding with my brother's bike until the same call came to me and my mates, wine, women and song once again won the day. The bike was left in the garage unceremoniously to rust.

A long time had past before I looked at it again, many years, and by now I was in my thirties. I dug it out and decided it was fit to ride to work with a bit of oil and grease. This probably rekindled my interest in cycling and during the holidays once a year my workmates and I made a pilgrimage on our bikes to Southport and back for the day, a distance of some 40 miles or so.

I was married by now with two boys who also had bikes so I persuaded my wife, not a cyclist by any means, to buy one for family trips out. So far so good until one fine day my elder son swerved in front of his mother who took a tumble taking a nasty knock to her knee. She decided her cycling days were over really before they had begun and with my younger son preferring to play rugby that left just me and elder son to carry the flag.

This flag carrying however, did not last long since some 'nice' person broke into the garage and nicked all the bikes, except mine of course which he kindly left thrown in a hedge, obviously not good enough, well it must have been at least 40 years old! I was heartbroken.......... I couldn't even claim the insurance on it.

I soldiered on with the old Sun until arthritic joints eventually came knocking on my body and early retirement loomed both for me and the bike which was thrown to the 'knackers yard'..... I barely escaped. During this time I had operations and eventually my joints eased somewhat with the medication.

Physios at the hospital told me cycling was excellent for knee problems because of the non-load bearing exercise and since my son, the elder one, had left his mountain bike made by Townsend (which was a replacement for the stolen one) in the garage when he moved on, I decided to try it out. So I found myself from having no gears (my bike) to four gears (my brother's bike) now facing 27, riding this around the roads must be easy, or so I thought.

My first ride took me up Alma Hill a 12% (~1 in 8 in old money) hill not long but sharp. The bike may have been littered with gears but like the old Elswick it was also very heavy, I think the frame from the headset to the bottom bracket was made from an old drainpipe the diameter was that large and to back up my argument some bloke from a cycling forum quoted; "Townsend is a cheap and nasty home shopping catalogue brand" I won't argue with that.

I set off at the bottom of the hill but within 15 yards or so I was soon out of breath with my heart pounding. There was a turn off to the left and gratefully I took it. Slowly I regained my composure and heart rate but turning right at the next corner I was once again confronted with another enormous hill but this time, however, 'spectators' lined the route. They were past pupils at the school where I previously worked and obviously I needed to make this to look easy. To say I nearly died with a smile on my face is an understatement but I made it to the top glad that I had not eaten dinner.

I persevered with the mountain bike but not for long it was just too cumbersome, so on the advice from my son and friends I went out to buy a racer to continue my training. I went to the local bike shop and was shocked to find the price of the new breed of road bikes. I only wanted a starter bike on the off chance I didn't take to it or it didn't take to my knees. The shop owner pointed me to his colleague on the other side of town who sold less well appointed bikes, I bought one, a yellow Tiger made in the sweat shops of Hungary but they were careful to put on the rear fork, hand built in Gt. Britain!

I needn't have worried about taking to it though, ducks and water springs to mind, I was hooked. The more I rode the more I enjoyed it and so I started thinking of longer and longer journeys, Blackpool became favourite, about 80 miles and my son became my pacer for the day. By now I had upgraded my yellow peril to a red Focus with much better specifications. I was now in business.

I planned the route meticulously to include minor roads with little traffic. This using Google maps took me an age cross referencing it with the Ordnance Survey Get-A-Map website. Finally I had the route and apart from travelling major roads going into Preston it was eminently suitable. One final touch was to travel the route by car with my nearest and dearest to check all was well, it was, and my son and I made Blackpool one August Bank Holiday Sunday 2006.

The weather was kind except for a westerly wind that tore at our faces off the Irish Sea. The only bad thing was my son falling off his new very expensive bike in St Annes after hitting the kerb whilst turning around to see if I was still in shouting distance. No injuries except pride and a gouged pedal which replacing it would probably have cost more than my Hungarian bike!

We made it to the Central Pier and the banana sandwiches tasted wonderful beneath the Tower but all too soon it was time to return. I had planned a circuitous route from Preston to Blackpool then back home. The way back through Blackpool took in the side streets one funnily enough being Palatine Road which consisted of boarding houses one of which was where my family and I used to holiday in the summer when I was a nipper.

It was an uneventful journey on the way back apart from me being extremely tired. The ride lasted 6 hr 20m 39s with a distance of 80.37 miles over a mainly flattish plain with a bump at the beginning, Appley Bridge and one at the end, Ashurst Beacon both long drawn out hills. We called at the Prince William pub at the top of the Beacon and a pint never tasted so good. I was elated with my time and the way that I finished, eighty miles was far more than I had ever done before and although an average of 12.6 mph left a lot to be desired, in football parlance; 'I was over the moon John'.

Having read the biographies of Marco 'the Pirate' Pantani and Sir Chris Hoy it was obvious their passion for the sport shone out from a very early age; mine I suppose, was a more platonic relationship with cycling, but a true love nonetheless. However, I did have a passion in my later years, apart from the marital type and that was for long distance walking with another teacher from school.

It all started with a friend Steve, a fell runner, who decided to attempt the Calderdale Hike with Duke of Edinburgh pupils and some staff. I of course volunteered because at that time I was cycling to school, jogging at lunch time and keeping myself reasonably fit. My medical condition, arthritis, had calmed down and I was in some sort of remission so I was taking advantage of a pain free body. The hike consisted of thirty odd miles across some of west Yorkshire's moors around March time, bleak was an understatement.

After enjoying this in a funny sort of way, blisters notwithstanding, I attempted many more for many years with Colin who was a member of the LDWA, a long distance walking association. During this time I found myself in the local library choosing books when by chance I let upon Wainwright's book of the Coast to Coast walk, St. Bees in Cumbria to Robin Hood's Bay in Yorkshire. What a challenge that would be, Colin and I travelling the byways of the north of England with the sun in our faces and the wind at our backs unfortunately it never came about; enter stage left arthritic knees, the 'lurgy' was back.

This was the time, as mentioned earlier, when the bike was ditched and I retired from school not long after. I recount this tale, for the Coast to Coast came back to haunt me after the Blackpool trip but this time by bike. I thought over and over of what to do next in long rides, a trip to Morecambe in a day seemed just too far and North Wales seemed just too difficult, with hills and mileage. The C2C seemed ideal, done over a number of days it would become an adventure exploring areas on the bike I had never been before.

I set about planning the route. There was of course Wainwright's but that was for walkers over the fells. Since there are a few acceptable ways to cross the country by bike a favourite had to be found. I went for Wainwright's start and finish ie. St. Bees to Robin Hood's Bay but by road rather than fell and moor. There is a planned route along the road, well sign posted so this I took with certain alterations to make it personal to me. Once again Google maps and the Get-A-Map website proved invaluable but even so it took me a number of months to get the route I wanted but finally I was there.

Now for the sleeping arrangements, having decided on the route it was simple to just say 40 miles or so a day, for it was meant to be a holiday and then find a pub for the night at that point. I wanted pubs rather than hotels or B & Bs for the atmosphere and the local chat. It all worked out fine with some great hostelries on the way.

The bike riding was terrific, different views and different terrain everyday gave me an appetite for long rides. The fells of Cumbria gave way to the north Penines and then the Yorkshire Dales finishing with the Yorkshire Moors. It was done over 5 days with my cycling son, with his girlfriend and my wife as back up in the car.

My plan over the north York Moors on the last two days was to keep the distances short because of the steep hills. However, a change of thought, (feeling strong but must have been weak in the head!) meant we did the last two days in one so we could rest at the last pub for the night and have a drink or three then go home in the morning hopefully not too worse for wear rather than straight after the ride. A good idea on paper, however in reality it was a nightmare with some exhausting steep climbs.

Over Kildale Moor at West Ho was the first hill a 1 in 4 then three 1 in 4s at Castleton followed by a 1 in 5 at Low Wood. At the next hill in the village of Grosmont the scene seemed so surreal, we stopped for a drink to take it in. It was like a Bank Holiday Monday in Blackpool, holidaymakers milling around a 1950s British Railways station waiting for the steam train to arrive all laughing and having a good time.

Simon and I could only look at the hill rising in front of us with held breath, our next piece of pain. It went straight up from the station on the North Yorkshire Moors Railway and was as steep as the previous hills but straight, the worst kind, with a bend near the top and crowds to contend with like the F1 spectators waiting for a crash, only these were hoping to see us get off and push as they probably would have to do, am I being paranoid? However, we didn't give them the pleasure but we did have a sly rest around the bend at the top.

The Sleights came next another 1 in 4 then The Cliffe at Ugglebarmby, the last one thank goodness. This started off as a 1 in 4 then for the remaining mile about 1 in 6 but the one which took the biscuit was the aptly named Limber Hill an unbelievable 1 in 3 ($33^{1/3}$ %). In between of course there were hills just short of the chevron class say 1 in 8 or so.

Were we glad to reach the top and make our way down to Robin Hood's Bay and after dipping front wheels in the North Sea and a cooling ice cream it was back to the Fox and Hounds for a well earned beverage.

During the late afternoon we were handed our surprise trophies by the back up team, a personal mug for me, with the route and date and a bowl for my son in the red and white polkadots of Le Tour's King of the Mountains, he thoroughly deserved it. A few beers were sunk that night I can tell you to the memory of a wonderful bike ride, a foretaste of bigger and better things to come.

Foreword

It was 2007 when I finished the C2C with Simon and for the next two years I continued to ride around my own locale enjoying the scenery and the rides especially in the summer but I became restless once again, what to do what to do? It was at this time I read a book that would focus my thinking, "French Revolutions" by Tim Moore, a fantastically funny read about a rank amateur cycling the Tour de France.

This had me thinking of my next big ride, not Le Tour but for me it had to be Le JO'G. Perhaps sometimes I thought out loud for my wife bought me a book of the route for my birthday, in the summer of 2009. Well that was it, wasn't it? I checked the route onto the new Anquet mapping web site I had found, which maps the whole of the country in Ordnance Survey maps. This was most enjoyable but took an absolute age to do.

Having done this I noticed that it was a roundabout route although there were alternatives on bigger roads. Not good enough I needed better direction, this I got from the CTC organization, The Cyclists Touring Club. I sent off for information and received a great package containing 3routes of varying types:

- Scenic route with Hostels
- Scenic Route with B&Bs
- A Fast Track route on larger roads

The route I finally decided upon from the ones I had seen was the Fast Track (Fast…ha!) from the CTC organisation. I chose this for a number of reasons:

1. It would be easy to spot road signs on bigger roads moving quickly (well reasonably quickly).
2. The roads would be better surfaced than minor roads.
3. The roads would also be easy to spot on the map and easier to get through the cities.
4. There would not be as many big hills on major roads as minor ones.
5. I would not get any punctures or very few hopefully, because of cleaner surfaces.

I set up the route on the Anquet website and printed two sets of A4 sheets of the journey, one set for my lady wife, the itinerant outside caterer who made the journey much easier to cope with, and one for me to be placed in my map wallet for each day, which was then attached to my handlebars. I found the wallet, a great buy, in Poundland no less and it served me exceptionally well, apart from when riding in the sheeting rain, and all for the princely sum of £1.

My ideas above worked well on the whole, with only a few blips but I have to say however, cycling the length of Britain, the road surfaces on our 'A' roads left a lot to be desired! On some roads, mainly in the North of England and Scotland, it was akin to riding on pebbledash not comfortable for me (my backside and shoulders mainly) or my bike. I now understand the travails of cyclists on the cobbles in Belgium.

Of course it was imperative that Mary became my back up for to do it 'Commando style' carrying your own equipment etc., was not an option, although I agreed with Ed Milliband's sentiments when he was asked about having a religion, "Not really but I have every admiration for those that do." The planning of the trip took the best part of 12 months, drawing routes, checking B &Bs then booking and confirming.

One hotel, the Mortimer's Cross, informed me two weeks before the off, that it had been sold and there was no room at the Inn, so to speak and since Mary didn't fancy the stable we needed to find other accommodation pronto! Fortunately The Corners Inn in the small village of Kingsland, just down the road, came to our rescue. Public Houses were chosen in the main for lunch stops as it was easier to find their postcodes for Mary to use on the sat nav and possibly drinks.

I decided that 60 to 70 miles a day was do-able but obviously I had to train for that in all weathers. I became interested in taking up one of my heroes, Jacques Anquetil's suggestion of training, when asked to outline his regimen for aspiring cyclists he replied, "A few whiskeys, blonde cigarettes, and a good woman," but my back up driver took a dim view of that, so plan B then. As an avid watcher of cricket, I took up the great Sir Ian Botham's philosophy of training; if you are a bowler you just bowl to get fit, simple as that. Forget the gym and all the periphery, bowl, bowl and bowl again, therefore as a cyclist, I thought, you cycle, cycle and cycle some more.

So starting slowly during the autumn of 2009 I cycled as much as I could building up the mileage more from January 2010. During the summer I was doing in the region of 200+ miles a week putting in one or more 60 odd miles, rain or shine. As in marathon training you never actually run a marathon I thought I wouldn't have to do the 400+ miles in a week in my training.

My main aim over the 15 days or so was to enjoy the ride and keep my eyes open to the ever changing scenery, from the rolling hills of the south to the craggy peaks of Scotland. It was never intended to be a head down and go ride, getting good averages and fast times, as it turned out it was a good decision. However, the length of the British Isles threw up all sorts of different weather and terrain. So that on some days it simply was head down and perhaps not go so much, as do battle against the topography and elements.

I decided the journey down would be in two parts, one to the village of Box near Bath, famous for the Box railway tunnel built under the direction of Brunel in the 1830s, staying for a couple of days at Simon's house, the cyclist and then on to Cornwall 'fit and ready' to start on the 26th July. The cycle ride itself was to include two rest stops, one back in Box, to celebrate my birthday (of 63 years) with elder son Simon and family and one at home to replenish and wash kit and say hello to younger son Robert and family.

George and Haydn, cycling friends of mine, who accompanied me on some of my training rides, had decided to share the pain on the leg, in George's case literally (more of that later), from home to Oxenholme, a mini adventure of their own and glad I was of their company. From there it would then be eight straight days of cycling through Scotland; I figured I would have ridden into fitness by then……… only time would tell.

Day Before

Saturday 24th July Box

Having arrived at Box on the Friday night and with my departure for Cornwall a day or so away I was confident my training had gone well. I bathed in the luxury of not sitting on my blade of a saddle for two days. Simon gave me all the tips, of course, for he is a reader of all things cycling, remember to 'Savlon' up each day on skin that will come into contact with the seat, I won't go into reasons why, it seems far too much information. Make sure you have enough fluids, enough food......"Enough, enough," I said "I'm ready", however, I should have listened more closely for as it transpired dear reader, I wasn't.

I relaxed and stretched my legs on the day before the off, sat in the sunshine and in the modern parlance, 'chilled out'. A 21 page dossier, developed by the Metropolitan Police but also used by other forces, gave three pages over to advice on the sorts of foods that police cyclists should eat. Among the recommendations are "high sugar spreads such as jam, honey and lemon curd." It goes on to state that these "should be eaten with a bread-based unsweetened item", anyone for jam butties then?

Anyway I decided to go against the Met's advice and take one bottle of energy (electrolyte) drink and one bottle of water for refreshment plus bits of food to be consumed throughout the day, mainly fruit and grain type biscuits. It has been said there is too much sugar in the energy drinks but at the risk of my teeth falling out I decided to take them along, I needed all the help I could get. Lunch would be supplied by my trusty outside caterer, Mary, of whom I have to say did me proud even in some of the more inhospitable places producing grand meals of banana sandwiches, pasta, beans just about everything including copious cups of coffee for the caffeine.

I suppose it is time to try to give you a feeling of what I must have looked like as I cycled the highways and byways of Great Britain. Firstly the bike, the most important piece of kit, is a red Focus Variado, made in Germany. It has been with me for four years (since August 2006) and has carried me over hill and dale for over 9000 miles with only punctures to contend with, although I have fallen off it three times, twice on slippery surfaces with leaves and ice, and once through the dreaded cleats, my early inexperience. With my yellow bike I could manage to loosen my feet from the toe clips before I hit the floor if a problem arose but being locked to the pedal took some getting used to especially at traffic lights!

I also carried with me a small bag fitted beneath the saddle containing a puncture repair kit and fresh tubes etc. for obvious emergencies although I would have been struggling with Eugene Christophe's problem on Le Tour in 1913. On the descent of Tourmalet 14km from the bottom his front forks snapped, so he picked up his bike and ran down to the bottom to a forge. Using his blacksmith skills he managed to fit them back together under the eagle eye of the race officials who were not happy he got help from a local boy on the bellows. Having finished his repair he still came in under two hours behind the leader!

The Variado is very well appointed with Shimano 105 gearing and brakes with Shimano wheels and a set of new Schwalbe Blizzard tyres for the journey. It has a triple chain wheel with a 9 cassette at the rear, one of the sprockets having 32 teeth which I'm sure will come in very handy throughout the trip especially in Scotland. The bike minus the front wheel, saddle and post managed to fit in the boot of the car with the rest of the luggage and cycling paraphernalia for the journey down to Cornwall. Talking of luggage I have to say that my cycling clothing has changed since buying my yellow bike to the present day.

Not wanting to look the part as I was unable to act it in those early days, I dressed down from a boy racer to baggy shorts that would outshine Sir Stanley Matthews and a loose cycling shirt that would flap about like a sail on the Cutty Sark. Now of course, I am able to hold my own with other geriatrics on bikes and so whilst it is still not exactly skin tight Lycra my clothing reflects a more streamline look suitable for the long and winding road. My black cycling helmet was a stipulation from my dear wife my concession to health and safety.

The route as I have previously said comes from the CTC organisation and moves up the western side of England with a touch into the south east of Wales, not enough for my liking, and then the west coast of Scotland. It will be well over 900 miles in length with more or less three times the ascent and descent of Mount Everest since I will be going from sea to shining sea, with 15 days cycling and then of course the two rest days. It would have been nice to make it a round two weeks on the bike but I rather fancied doing only a few miles on the last stage to be reasonably fit for the finish and its accompanying revelry. It has been said about the other longish bike ride in France that the race is won or lost in the second week when they attack the Pyrenean mountains and the Alps can this be true for me in the wilds of Scotland on my second week with five to six hours struggle up the Highlands some days?

Prologue

Sunday 25th July Box to St. Just

Finally the day dawned, Sunday 25th July. This is the day I set off for St. Just, my last hold up before the trip proper, the weather is cloudy but dry and warm. Did I sleep well last night? Not really, with the copious glasses of wine the previous night and the excitement. I did, however, experience a wonderful egg, bacon and toast breakfast with fresh coffee, starting already with the caffeine.

After the food I checked the Metcheck website on weather for the next three days, changeable, oh good. The car was packed up with luggage and bike and we were off after setting sat nav for the Commercial Hotel in St. Just Cornwall, the butterflies, moths and every other flying insect I could think of took wing as the car pulled away from the kerb, the journey as far as I was concerned started now.

We moved from Box to the M4 then the M5 towards Bristol, a pretty uneventful journey except for the Mendip Hills looming large on the horizon, gulping, I realised I would be back over them soon enough. The M5 took us down to Exeter where we picked up the A30 to Penzance. Now I remember the CTC explaining about the dangers of cycling to Exeter along the A30, I could now see what they meant. Even so it did not deter some game or should I say stupid folk from cycling on, what appeared to be a, very narrow cycle path or was it just a white line at the side of the road? The traffic was hurtling past at 60+ mph, extremely large continental trucks with better suction than a Dyson, lives or at the very least limbs were obviously at risk.

From the edge of Dartmoor, an area I would get to know well later, we made our way over Bodmin moor and I have to say the views were, if we are to continue with a French theme of cycling, magnifique. With such vistas I remembered a phrase attributed to Oscar Wilde, so with apologies to him I thought that 'I may be riding in the gutter but I would still be looking at the stars'. However, all good things must come to an end and we left Bodmin before dropping down towards Penzance where David, the sat nav voice informed us to take the right hand fork to St. Just. Once again the scenery was beautiful but a bit too up and down for my liking.

We entered the town from the east and turned into the square or to be more geometrical, the triangle. There was a pub on each of the three sides, ours being the Commercial Hotel on the first we came to. St. Just was originally the centre of the tin mining industry on this peninsula, the streets of granite cottages seemed to reflect the hard days of mining past.

Having registered in the hotel and deposited the luggage in our room we set off for Land's End to check out the start for the day after. I remembered from the original route book that Mary bought me that St. Just was on this route or at least close by and as I descended a great hill was I glad I chose to go another way. When we arrived at the car park area for Land's End we were informed of the price to park, £4 no matter how long you stayed, welcome to Cornwall and rip off Britain, needless to say we didn't stay and drove around the roundabout back out again much to the dismay of the parking attendant. £4 for the car park seemed a bit steep but unfortunately that is where the signpost was so we resigned ourselves to having to pay it in the morning for a mere matter of minutes which did not go down well.

Time was moving on and the call of food was becoming stronger so we went back up the hill to St. Just, thankfully I would be on a much flatter road to Penzance the next day. On the way back I was thinking about the ride in the morning, in fact I had not stopped thinking about it for a long time, when my stomach seemed to drop to my knees, water bottles bought specially for the job, where are they? I remembered Simon's checks back at Box. My mind was in a whirl I could not remember seeing them anywhere in the car the reason being I'd forgotten to pack them, how could I have been so stupid? Friends who know me well will tell you that is simple for me, a good memory not being my strong point!

I read somewhere that in the dark and distance past of the Tour de France the riders would not necessarily carry bidons but make large scale attacks on bars en route to wipe them out of beer, spirits, champagne the lot to drink on the way. I can't quite see the Pig and Whistle, King's Arms et al along the route allowing that to go on for me somehow, so another plan was needed. Thankfully, Mary (I knew I had brought her for a reason) calmed me down and suggested I go to the local store to stock up on bottle water for the first part of the journey and since the lunch stop was at the Sainsbury's supermarket tomorrow I could replace them for the real thing, what good organisation!

The water bottles of course would not fit perfectly into the cages on my bike, one was squashed and the other was loose having been clever and bought both sizes, typical. However, they would have to do, any port in a storm or more accurately any bottle for a bike.

We ate and drank our fill in the local hostelries and tomorrow the adventure would begin, was it possible for a 62 year old man to feel so much excitement?

It was a rainy Rotterdam that hosted the prologue time trial of the 2010 Tour de France and a race that, in the end, confounded many pre-race predictions. Except one, Fabian Cancellara (Saxo Bank). The Swiss time trial specialist, was the winner, beating the long-time leader Tony Martin (HTC-Columbia) to claim his fourth Tour prologue.

What had been billed beforehand as a straightforward, non-technical course over 8.9km, was made far more testing, and infinitely more dangerous, by the rain that fell consistently throughout. Only the final wave of starters were spared the incessant drizzle, as the sun emerged and the roads dried to allow some of the big hitters a much more comfortable run than the earlier starters.

Cancellara blasted around the 8.9km in a time of 10:00 min. It was a perfect ten, as he pointed on the podium. With Martin a further ten seconds back and David Millar (Garmin-Transitions) third at 10:20.

Behind Cancellara, though, the results sheet made for fascinating and intriguing reading, partly perhaps, as a consequence of the conditions.

Stage 1

I'm off, well at least I'm up. Washed then shaved although I resisted the legs as I didn't think that would make much difference to the drag, dressed and down for an early breakfast before any other resident stirred. Banana, cereal and a full English followed by toast and marmalade fuelled the Forrester machine in readiness for the day. I can't help thinking this is not what Stephen Roche would have had in 1987 when he won the famous race across the Channel.

Apart from the excellent breakfast it was a dismal start to the day, a hanging mist cloaked the village and threatened drizzle. Any other time a look out of the window and you would have gone back to bed but not today because today was the day I had been dreaming about for over 12 months. We packed up the luggage and transferred the bike to the car and finally we were on our way to Land's End. The ride begins.

Down the hill from St. Just and into the Land's End car park a bonus when we arrived, nobody there to collect the £4, just a pay and display....ha some hope, the little man wins again. Mary was dispatched to find the finger post while I sorted out the bike, equipment and kit. For some reason I was having great difficulty in getting ready all fingers and thumbs. Eventually I'm set but then I have lost the car keys, would you believe it? Yes. I looked everywhere and finally after cursing and

31

shouting, they were in my pocket. Mary was a beacon of calm as always and we made our way to the abysmal apology for a signpost. I found out later that the original post, combined with its plot of land it sits upon had been sold, so the photographer could make a fast £10 a photo from gullible tourists. However this post did not seem to be available, nowhere to be found, do they take it up at night to avoid people actually taking their own photographs, surely not. Well the apology for one would have to do. Photos duly taken I made my way to the off, now for the ride.

After forgetting water bottles, losing car keys what else could go wrong, surely nothing? The sat nav was set up from Mary's map book a quick kiss for good luck and she's off. I jumped on the bike, readied myself, deep breath, took in the surroundings tried to stem the butterflies still in my stomach, looked down at the map...what map? In my best Shaggy's voice from Scooby Do "Yikes!" or something similar, nothing was wrapped around my handlebars. A quick panicky phone call halted Mary almost a mile away, thank heavens for mobile phones. Nerves, it had to be nerves hadn't it? I would get better organised, wouldn't I?

Now having actually ridden in earnest on a Cornish road, albeit a bit quick to take in the surroundings, I felt a great buzz of excitement. Reaching Mary parked at the side of the road about a mile away the sun began to shine through the mist and the blue sky started to appear, must be an omen of good things to come. Having settled my map wallet on my bike I was now ready for the off and off I went as Mary disappeared in the distance hoping that the next time I saw her would be in Truro.

After a few miles of cycling I stopped to switch on my MP3 player to keep me company when 5 or 6 cyclists, in a group with charity type T-shirts, passed by with a hearty greeting. I got to thinking why not use them as a wind shield and for pace, good idea. I caught up with them, which was not all that easy but I was full of adrenaline by now, and sat on their coat tails. Pretty soon I got the feeling the back marker of the group was not a happy bunny, he turned around constantly to check my whereabouts.

This put me in mind of a fell race I once took part in many years ago with my good friend Steve, an excellent and experienced runner. He twigged that the man behind was simply using us as a 'map' Steve, ever the pro was not happy, I personally couldn't care less so when we got out of sight at the next rocky outcrop he told me to run like hell to lose him which I did, we lost him and I think half my stomach contents as well!

The back marker may have had the same idea as Steve and transferred the message along to his companions or they were just too quick because the first hill we came to I found myself alone and panting like a dog in a desert. Still I was happy enough with my own company, singing along to the Beatles coming through my earphones.

Just before Newlyn and Penzance I followed the old A30, thankfully not the trunk road towards Exeter but a much less busier road which took me down to the coast, I then skirted Penzance and headed out into the country towards Redruth. Considering it was my first day I was making good time despite the wind however, which I hoped would be SW blowing me home being NW blowing me back and was constantly in my face all the way to the first stop, the Sainsbury's supermarket in Truro. You will find reading this book that I am not over enamoured with wind especially in the wrong direction. I picked up the A390 dual carriageway for a few miles, a bit of a pain but being so close to lunch I put the traffic to the back of my mind. I had done well on the first leg to lunch, keeping up a good average and no problems with the terrain.

At the supermarket I ate my fill of banana 'butties' and lovely pasta Mary had bought and prepared, washed down with lashings of coffee. The weather by now was warm with a sunny blue sky, this trip should be a doddle but remember the old adage; pride goes before a fall, never a true word was spoken and not for the first time this trip. I made my way into the supermarket to buy new water bottles did I look a picture, togged up for Le Tour in my pretend lycra, I suppose I could have been confused as the latest Gok of fashion! I searched high and low for water bottles, none to be found.

In desperation I asked a member of staff whilst trying to cover up my lack of fashion sense on a Monday afternoon shopping. With an interesting look he directed me to the children's section that held sandwich boxes etc! There I found the bottles amongst the Spidermen and Supermen lunch boxes, now they *would* look good on the bike but fortunately I managed to find some black translucent ones which would have to do until I got home and replaced them with 'adult' ones. It could have been worse, they could have been adorned with the Simpsons! Lance would have been impressed.

Back to the car I said to Mary only 35 miles to go, a snip, see you in Liskeard, at the Hotel Nebula. So with a cheery goodbye I'm off again through Truro not knowing what was to follow. In normal circumstances back home, 35 miles would take me no longer than $2^1/_2$ hours, unfortunately I did not count on the A390 being the hilliest road in Christendom a bit of a nightmare, I ended up going slower and slower, my average for the day ruined for ever.

Moving away from Truro I crossed the Tresillian river and went back out into the country were my nightmare began. The road seemed to take on the appearance of the world's longest roller coaster with a couple of Blackpool Big Ones thrown in. The scenery of course was wonderful but could only be viewed when taking a food/drink/rest stop and even then through squinty eyes as the sun turned Cornwall into desert conditions baking in the heat of the afternoon.

Through St. Austell I approached my longest hill of the trip so far, from St. Blazey to Penpillick a distance just short of 2 miles. I stopped for a drink. In changing my map sheets over my heart sank as there was an extra sheet I hadn't noticed, meaning at least another 7 miles after the hill! This was a low time for me and it was only on the first day, could it get any worse? The answer came in the affirmative later outside Liskeard.

Back to the here and now there was a hill to contend with. I was so hot and now miserable I needed to do this for my own peace of mind and eventually after fighting the diesel smoke from an old wagon in front of me vying for position, I eventually made it, too tired to punch the air, I just trundled along following the roller coaster.

Through Lostwithiel I finally found myself on the outskirts of Liskeard looking down onto the busy

A38. I phoned Mary to tell her of my whereabouts and my close proximity to the finish when she deflated me with the news that the hotel was closed and she was attempting to find an alternative. I thought back to my organising days and remembered finding the hotel on Google Streetview. There was a police car in the street with groups of people milling around, perhaps the penny should have dropped as to the nature of the area.

Riding down to meet the A38 I crossed the road to gain access to the cycle lane when a stray dog caught my attention, not good for cyclists are stray dogs. Another police car moved into view with the intention of catching the said stray, the policeman needless to say had the same luck as I had with the town and hotel. The dog set off down the cycle lane like the Littlest Hobo leaving the policeman doing a double teapot by the side of his car.

When I eventually arrived in Liskeard and Mary showed me the hotel, it did not quite do its webpage justice, situated as it was in a less than salubrious part of town! The car park around the back seemed a great meeting place for dogs and people to smash glass bottles its detritus gave it a derelict look, hardly welcoming. A message attached to the front door on a piece of paper invited callers to knock on the cottage next door if the hotel was closed and after knocking, so was the cottage what a way to run a business.

However, a woman, who lives over the road from the hotel, had spoken to Mary during the afternoon informing her that the landlord had let this place go but she did point out there was a Premier Inn close by to which we shot off by car after loading up the bike.

"Full up," was the reply when I asked for a bed for the night. The receptionist offered alternatives but none were suitable.

"How about Sue's?" I asked, she being a friend from the Plymouth area.

"Good Idea," replied Mary, we phoned,

"No problem," we went.

So we set the sat nav for Brixton a little village just outside of Plymouth arriving there to a 'hero's welcome' in the late afternoon. After a good hot shower and a change of clothes I was ready for the afternoon Gordons. Later we had a lovely lamb casserole with red wine and for me copious glasses of water, sat in the evening sun in the good company of friends, for George, my cycling friend and his family were also staying there.

The nightmare of the day became a distant memory as the wine and the tiredness took over and so with a full stomach and a happy heart I retired to my bed, dreaming of the pleasures of the next day, which were Dartmoor, more hills and after the evening weather forecast, rain leaving the rest of the company to their wine and conversation.

The Tour de France hasn't even reached the feared cobblestones and massive crashes have already taken down the majority of the peloton, but one rider who has the well-demonstrated ability to dodge the bullets, Alessandro Petacchi, claimed the stage victory.

The Lampre-Farnese Vini sprinter, who also successfully avoided a dramatic Tour de Suisse crash to win there last month, took his first Tour stage win since his record Grand Tour run of 2003. Petacchi bested HTC-Columbia's Mark Renshaw and Thor Hushovd (Cervelo TestTeam) after a crash stopped several of the top sprinters in the final bend, including Mark Cavendish (HTC-Columbia) and Oscar Freire (Rabobank).

"It was a special finale. In the last turn, everybody came
in fast and nobody wanted to brake, so there was a crash and a lot of confusion. I did a very risky sprint. I attacked from far out, despite the head wind and the false-flat road," Petacchi said.

"I think I've done a great sprint. I'm not sure that Cavendish would have beat (sic) me if he'd been there at the end because I've really done a great sprint."

Le JO'G Stage 1 2010		Le Tour Stage 1 2010
Land's End - Liskeard		Rotterdam - Brussels
		Winner Petacchi
Distance	75.853 miles	139.69 miles
Time Cycling	5hr.34m.58s.	5hr.9m.38s.
Average Speed	13.6 mph.	27.07 mph.

Stage 2

Tuesday 27th July Liskeard to Uffculme

Not quite up at the crack of dawn and legs felt tired. Should have taken the advice of George's son Paul, the physio, to have had an ice bath when I arrived yesterday but would you? Anyhow I will just have to get on with it, I was sure the adrenaline would see me through if not the red wine of last night. Breakfast was a lazy affair but this time more on the poached eggs than the full English. After lots of chat, time marched on and reluctantly we had to say our goodbyes and set off back to the 'wonderful' Liskeard and the Hotel Nebula.

When organising the hotels I talked to John, the owner of the hotel, over the phone trying to get him to confirm the booking via e-mail, he was certainly not with the new technology or perhaps he was not just with anything or do we do him a disservice and caught him on a bad day, who knows? Back in the town outside the hotel whilst retrieving my bike from the back of the car I spied a lone figure emerging from the Nebula, a walker, I wondered how he went on, I hope he enjoyed himself as much as we did last night but somehow I doubted it.

Having replaced the wheel and saddle my trusty bike was ready for the off but not me yet. I kitted myself out in my cycling gear and had something to eat. Mary left in the car and then it started to drizzle, Billinge rain must have followed me down. I put my rain jacket on, leg over the crossbar and then realised I had no gloves or any food for the journey, a déjà vu moment, obviously I needed to concentrate more at the start of these rides. I decided, as it turned out wrongly, that I would be able to manage until the dinner stop somewhere on Dartmoor. The rain then abated as quickly as it started, so I removed the rain jacket and packed it away in its little pouch, not an easy process simply folding it in your hands then I made my way out of Liskeard onto the Tavistock road.

Sue had told me last night about Liskeard not being the best Cornwall has to offer and it felt good to be leaving, for it had done nothing to endear itself to us. Sorry you Likeardians perhaps I'll see you in a better light in the future. I was off to Tavistock a lovely market town, although the proper market day was Friday today's fayre was bric-a-brac and crafts, the route was by way of the now infamously well known hilly A390. It did not let me down.

Sue told me of the hills the previous night but I was there before her for when I checked the route in the preliminary organisation, I looked on the Google Earth website of the area, it was not a happy picture. I remembered viewing the road on the computer and writing on the map;
Hill, Hilly, Very Hilly, Extremely Hilly, One Long Hill with Steep Bits and so on.
I decided then, it might be better not knowing the future so I stopped checking but now I am here………. gulp.

The drizzle descended once more, so the rain jacket adorned my shoulders yet again, I swore not to be taken off in the foreseeable future. The road again became a Big Dipper of a ride all the way to the town of Gunnislake, with another hill but fortunately it was 12%

40

going down through the town. At the bottom I think my brakes would have melted had it not been for the incessant drizzle cooling both them and me down, however, on a lighter note the bunting was out, could it be for me I mused, they must have heard about my trip…..mmmm.

I continued over the river at the bottom and geographically speaking if there is a river valley, after the down there must be an up, there was. Looking at my map there were two ways to attack this hill, the gung ho way straight up with a chevron marked on the map (remember at least 1 in 7) or the twisting turning way of the Italian job, guess which one I chose? Wrong, I chose the second one. As I made my way rounding the curves it reminded me of the duel between Pantani and Armstrong on Ventoux in 2000 during the Tour but am I perhaps overstating my prowess to put me in such vaulted company, not at all.

These climbs eventually saw me riding into 'Tavvy' as the locals call it, the lovely market town on the border of Cornwall and Devon but it was seemingly less so in the rain which got heavier by the minute, leaving my map harder to see which made my navigation increasingly more difficult, because of this I wandered around for a bit, apologies to Hamlet cigars, but eventually I found the route a right hand fork the B3357 going upwards. The road led out from an avenue of trees to the beginning of Dartmoor,

I stopped for a drink and to check the map with a large hill looming it was imperative I got the correct route. A cyclist coming down the hill stopped on the other side of the road in the pouring rain to check if I was lost or not, a nice gesture which was to happen more than once on the ride.

Well up I go, a 1 in 8 start with a 1 in 5 sting later, for what seemed like an absolute age, mind you the speed I was going it probably was! The rain came down now more in buckets than in a pour but I reached what must be the top for I saw a viewpoint marked on the map and cars in the car park with a van sporting the sign; Willy's Cornish Ice Cream strangely enough doing very little trade.

I stopped to allow lungs and heart to regain some modicum of control and looked at the view through rain spattered glasses, what did I see, mist and more mist, rain and more rain, I felt a little deflated after climbing for so long that the view was obscured by the extreme precipitation over the moor made famous by various authors and of course the prison.

I had been to Dartmoor once before, when on a school holiday we walked the moors and it rained then with nothing but a pacamac to keep me dry, nothing seemed to have changed in the last fifty years or so. When I walked the hills of the Lake District, on a ridge walk you could usually guarantee a flattish top which allowed some respite for your legs after the climb, not so on Dartmoor it seemed.

Up and down I went for miles, passing the turn off for Princetown, the home of the prison, my mind wondered whether it was better to be an inmate than a wet through biker at that moment. There could not have been a worse time to forget my gloves and biscuits, my hands were slipping on the wet handlebars and brakes, which didn't work too well anyway with the rain and I was relying only on my drink for energy, I was becoming a little weary and despondent. The road had turned into a river with rainwater gushing across from one side to another making the downhill section scarily difficult and slow, bang goes the average again!

I turned left on the B3212 to Postbridge and the rain began to ease somewhat giving me some help for the next 5 miles to the car park for lunch. I stopped at the top of a steep hill above the said car park and looked down for Mary, no car was to be seen, phone out.

"Hello," I said, "where are you?"

"At the car park," came the reply.

"Not the one marked on the map," I ventured.

"I didn't know which that was but this is a big one and there are coaches here."

I looked in the distance, for she must be ahead not having passed her and saw on the horizon of the next hill a couple of coaches and possibly a black Mondeo car. This of course meant another down and up before I ate, time to go.

I arrived at the car park with a very cold wind blowing across me and I couldn't wait to dismount and find a warm haven in the car but did food ever taste so sweetly, Mary had excelled herself in the lunch department, apart from there being no hot coffee, we forgot to make it at Sue's house in the morning, what a day to forget, a hot beverage would have gone down a real treat with a wee dram to warm the cockles.

I set off in much higher spirits than when I had landed even without the warming whisky, now fully kitted out with gloves and biscuits. On to the town of Moretonhampstead, thankfully all downhill and from the wilds of the moor I was cycling in leafy lanes away from the wind and now the rain had stopped I was feeling better already. More steep protracted hills came and went the last one being marked on my map as a long hill with a steep bit, Google Earth was not wrong. I went to change down to bottom gear to give myself a chance but found out I was already there, 'oh dear' I thought, nothing for it but to dance on my pedals like Alberto Contador in the Alps which lasted for all of about 10 seconds, so I sat back down on my seat and danced like John Sergeant in Strictly Come Dancing, less arduous, I slowed and plodded but eventually I made it.

I arrived at my first big city, Exeter the capital of Devon. Riding down to its river, the Exe my theory of choosing this route being able to spot roads and signs easier when travelling through cities was to be put to the test. It failed miserably at the first hurdle. After the river I suddenly lost all signs for the B3212, what to do what to do, the traffic was also unforgiving when coming into contact with a lost biker so I stopped, dismounted and a little disgruntled went into the nearest shop which sold books, stationery and maps, chances. I asked the lady shopkeeper,

"Is the road outside your shop the B3212?"

A perfectly reasonable question I thought, although Mary didn't quite think so when I told her about it later. The shopkeeper gave me a blank look and after a pause she replied very slowly,

"I have no idea."

At this point I was then hoping for the AA reply; but I know a man who does, it was not forthcoming.

However, she was most helpful in producing map after map of the city and eventually she managed to point me in the right direction but my memory failed me after the first couple of turns and I needed to ask again. One of our very helpful Community Policemen came to my rescue, it seemed I came off the road too soon. He directed me to a pedestrian area through the heart of the city which was a complete change from the country roads I had been following.

At the other side of Exeter I picked up the B3181 which took me north to the suburbs and the town of Broadclyst. I was stuck on this road shadowing and criss-crossing the M5 motorway through the towns of Cullompton and Willand the areas around which, provided me with very uninteresting countryside. The roads were by now much flatter and I was able to up my pace although tiredness was already creeping in. This road took me all the way to my first actual stay in a pub on the journey, the Waterloo Cross, just outside Uffculme and thankfully I managed to store the bike without dismantling it for the car.

The Waterloo Cross hotel is situated on the border between Devon and Somerset which meant, of course I had done three counties in two days, not bad going that. It also turned out to belong to the Marstons Brewery pub chain which was excellent news since Marstons bitter is a particular favourite of mine. Unfortunately for some strange reason it did not sell any Marstons beers, which seemed quite unbelievable and certainly bad news for me.

The manager turned out to be very amenable in storing the bike and the food in the evening certainly hit the spot. The room was enormous with lots of floor space to spread out my wet kit to dry making the place feel like a WI jumble sale. The bed was more than comfortable and after the problems of Liskeard it was good to be settled at night, although perhaps a little too early for Mary at half past eight, well I was tired, to sleep and dream of the morning with hopefully flatter roads and some sun on my back.

Spa is Belgium's home of speed - the city's world-renowned motor racing circuit has hosted daring feats over the decades - and there was plenty of bravado during today's 201km journey from Brussels to the Wallonne region, so it was fitting that a man known for his bravado takes line honours.

Quick Step's Sylvain Chavanel put in what will likely be one of the best performances of the this year's Tour de France - on just the third day of the event - to win in Spa and put himself in the maillot jaune *(Yellow Jersey) ahead of the race's entry to French soil, which will come during tomorrow's stage to Porte du Hainaut.*

The peloton, coming in nearly four minutes behind, failed to fulfil the city's need for speed, instead staging a 'go-slow' protest against the slippery descent with 30km to go.

Le JO'G Stage 2 2010		Le Tour Stage 2 2010	
Liskeard - Uffculme		Brussels - Spa	
		Winner Chavanel	
Distance	71.392 miles		125.63 miles
Time Cycling	6hr.10m.48s.		4hr.40m.48s.
Average Speed	11.6 mph.		26.84 mph.

Stage 3

Wednesday 28th July Uffculme to Pill

Today I left the steep and rolling hills of Devon and Cornwall and moved into the county of Somerset, in fact an area known as The Somerset Levels, sounded good to me! I slept reasonably well and was up early not surprisingly, following the age old maxim, early to bed and early to rise. We breakfasted at 7.30am amongst the travelling salesmen who made their way in a little later.

This must be a favourite haunt for Mondeo man (and woman in our case) situated as it was on the A38, the main route to the south west of England. As I looked out of the window the weather could not have been more different to the previous day over Dartmoor, the sun had definitely got its hat on and I was certainly coming out to play.

After breakfast we paid up, packed up and retrieved the bike from the linen store, I made sure this time nothing would be forgotten by involving Mary as a checklist. I lifted my aching legs onto the bike; the previous day's travelling up and down the hills had certainly taken its toll on my thigh muscles. A last check, my goodbyes to the dinner lady and I was off on the A38 to Wellington, Taunton and Bridgwater, who needed maps?

Five minutes in on these 'levels' I met a nice little 1 in 8 hill for about a quarter of a mile, that certainly got the legs, lungs and heart moving. From here on in the road was everything I could ask for, not too busy, lovely smooth surface and now lacking hills which allowed me to get up some speed, well into the 15s average, a real bonus and my muscle ache just slipped away in the morning sunshine now that's what I call the nearest thing to bike heaven.

Wellington, the first town, came up after about 9 miles with the Blackdown Hills to the south I was glad I was travelling through the valley. The town, apparently, gave its name to the famous 'Iron Duke', victor of the Battle of Waterloo and a 175ft column was erected on the scarp edge of the Blackdowns which I didn't see myself, probably because of my speed on the flattish roads, although I think the more likely answer was that it was too far away!

The next in the trilogy of towns on the A38 is Taunton, the county town of Somerset. This is another old market town completely covered in flowers, very pretty and a dream to get through, much more like it. For me it is famous for the racecourse and a plethora of great cricketers who played at Taunton for Somerset, Sir Ian Botham and Sir Viv. Richards to mention but two, I could go on but people say I'm boring.

However, moving on I arrived at Bridgwater at breakneck speed (poetic licence) another lovely old town with wonderful buildings. The Quantock hills are to the west of the town thankfully but unfortunately the Mendips are to the north, which is my direction. I stopped to have a drink outside The Steak House restaurant and noticed they were serving a meat feast platter, 'If You Dare Grill' consisting of 12 pieces of various meats and chips with mushrooms, peas, pineapple, onions, tomato, two fried eggs and coleslaw in an attempt to balance the nutritional value, 5256 calories the lot, I was tempted but could I get back on my bike? I took a healthier option and ate a strawberry fruit and grain biscuit instead with only just a little envy.

Just out of Bridgwater I picked up the A39 and crossed over the M5 again towards a hill, whatever happened to the levels? Going up the hill I started to chase two lady bikers, all togged up for a journey but suffering with the climb. I was jockeying for position, at the time, with a continental juggernaut, he wanted to pass but the road was too narrow so there was a bit of an impasse. Using the two cyclists as a hare I managed to overtake them and left them to the clutches of the foreign lorry.

Further on up the hill I heard a scream from behind, I presumed the driver had perhaps come too close for comfort for the women and not the worst case scenario, however, I managed to beat the 40 tonner to my turn off onto the B3141 although the hill continued there was now peace and quiet. Having reached the village of Woolavington I stopped at the side of the road to ring Mary to prepare for lunch when who should come past but the two ladies laughing and talking looking unscathed and quite sprightly after their ordeal. I wondered if they were also en route to John O'Groats and would our paths cross again.

I actually arrived at the dinner stop, the Crown Inn in East Huntspill before opening time, not good for lunch but great for morale. The journey had been quite wonderful so far with flattish roads and great views and I felt much stronger in my legs. The pub when I arrived, however, was having renovation work and was not conducive to good eating. Mary told me of a better one up the road apiece so we made for there. Lunch again was of a great variety, much impressed by the outside catering. All too soon though, I was on my way again, this time up more hills towards the Mendips, Cheddar and its famous Gorge.

I moved onto the B3139 just before the hamlet of Watchfield and from there it was just a joy to be on the road. The sun was shining and the road was empty of cars all the way to the village of Wedmore which had beautiful cottages lining the route, I could quite easily be slipping through the villages of France with sunflower fields on that other cycle ride. From Wedmore I turned north passing Cheddar town to my right with its reservoir on my left, then the smile on my face slipped as I looked ahead, the Mendips.

I recall my concern on the journey down it was not in vain, they were a great barrier of rock and vegetation across the road a ridge of enormous proportions getting bigger the closer I got. I stopped for refreshment and looked at the road moving up the hill, there was no get out clause this time the winding of bends like the ascent out of Gunnislake it was all or nothing. A quick look at the map proved me right it went straight up and over, I made my way to the bottom of the hill by way of a roundabout and started to ascend.

I settled into a rhythm like the famous Jan Ulrich (for the purists amongst you) winner of the 1997 Tour although he was the eternal second from then on. It was long certainly, but funnily enough nothing that I couldn't handle was I riding into fitness so soon? I made it to the top breathing hard, gasping for a drink and hungry but well satisfied with my climb in the sun. It was all down hill from here, literally but not yet metaphorically that came later, to Shipham the next town, wonderful. I was going northwards now on the B3133 it was mainly flattish quiet and I managed to keep up a good pace, however at the town of Yatton I started to veer northwest the wind being westerly was now more in my face, slow progress was made. I rode into the town of Clevedon then no progress, lost again.

Clevedon is an old Victorian seaside town with lots of dark stone houses not very uplifting to a tired lost lonely cyclist. In the town I had a choice of routes; to turn right onto the B3130 or to be more adventurous and find the cycle way south of the coast that runs parallel with the good old M5 motorway to the village of Pill or to be more precise the Fire Station in the village of Pill, my stopping point.

Which did I choose, never let it be said I'm not adventurous, the cycle way it was, what a terrible decision early on. This is the bit were I got lost and it looked so easy on the map, once again I needed to ask the locals for the direction to the cycle path. The first couple I asked,

"We're not from round here me dearie."

Ask again,

"No sorry I'm from Portishead."

I even asked a couple of workmen at the local Fire station who of course were also out of towners!

What is it with this place do they bus them in to make it look busy? At last I found a local, another workman this time at some road works, who put me on the correct path and eventually I was rolling along the Avon 10 route but in hindsight it probably would have been quicker to take the B3130 across country.

It was an exceptionally lovely route though with views to the sea and bowling along looking at these I was nearly run over by a car coming the other way! Some cycle route. I was shadowing the M5 motorway again for some time until the village of Clapton in Gordano, through the village the cycle way finished and I ended up looking at an enormous hill my heart dropped, for mentally my legs were close to the finish and did not need any setback, I was getting quite tired.

A quick stop to refresh parts even beer couldn't reach and I noticed the cycle way had crossed the road a little up the hill, aha! I moved on. From here another pleasant couple of miles found me slipping beneath the M5 and then just beyond Portbury, a full stop I reached the A369.

To say this was a busy road would have been an understatement of the highest magnitude akin to the Black Knight in the film Monty Python and the Holy Grail saying "It's just a flesh wound," after having both his arms cut off. There were lorries and trucks of all sizes making their way down to the docks at Portishead interspersed with cars, vans and any other vehicle you could think of with the exception of a push bike, that just did not register in the mind of the person who set up the cycle way, typical.

I managed after some considerable time and taking my life in my hands to cross this imitation of the M5 and thankfully did not have to wait long before the left turn to the village of Pill and its Fire Station. I chose the Fire Station as the stop for easy access away from the village onto the road to Box and Simon, just in case you were wondering. After getting lost again, unbelievably, I eventually arrived at the station thanks to a good lady who knew the way. I found Mary and packed away my bike for the drive back to Simon's and a beer, oh and that little thing, my birthday in the morning.

It had been a talking point for months and it delivered the spectacle for which everyone had hoped. Cobbles, crashes and a general sense of calamity again turned the Tour de France on its head during stage three after the previous three days had thrown their fair share of mishaps and surprises.

And while a Paris-Roubaix victory may have escaped Thor Hushovd over the years, Cervélo TestTeam's big Norwegian sprinter grabbed a fine consolation prize - a Tour stage win that took riders over sectors of pavé that turned the event's third stage, a 213km journey from Wanze to Arenberg Porte du Hainaut, into a miniature version of ASO's famed Spring Classic.

It had observers talking about the opening week of this year's Tour being one of the most exciting in years - certainly not formulaic - justifying the inclusion of the stage by the event's organisers. The end result was a new maillot jaune *in Fabian Cancellara, the Swiss rider reclaiming the jersey he lost during yesterday's confusion and controversy.*

Le JO'G Stage 3 2010		Le Tour Stage 3 2010
Uffculme - Pill		Wanze - Arenberg
		Winner Hushovd
Distance	68.148 miles	131.25 miles
Time Cycling	4hr.53m.16s.	4hr.49m.38s.
Average Speed	14.0 mph.	27.19 mph.

Rest Day 1

Thursday 29th July Box

I don't know exactly what the cyclists do on their rest days during the Tour, more than likely sweat on their turbo trainers or even dare I say go for a leisurely (if that is possible) bike ride, me I rested, remember Sir Ian and his philosophy it had worked for me thus far. So, well rested after the few wines the night before I awoke and slowly made my way down the stairs feeling all of my 63 years to the waiting arms of my lovely outside caterer with son Simon, his wife Katie and of course my lovely granddaughter Heidi waiting in the wings.

Traditionally before breakfast presents had to be opened, this birthday was no different to any other in the Forrester household. Sports drinks in powder form, both energy and recovery, with a few pairs of the ubiquitous cycling socks for the rest of the journey (you can never have enough) from the children. A great cycling gilet, red white and black to match my bike no less, which I'm sure will come in handy further north from Mary. Simon made his hasty departure for work and I set about the wonderful breakfast prepared for me containing, I'm in no doubt, a monstrous number of calories.

It was a beautiful day, weather wise, the sun shone and it was lovely and warm in the garden. I decided to repay the bike for a trouble free journey so far by giving it a good clean. Down to the car to get all the bike paraphernalia, oil, cleaning agents etc. and I was ready. The ladies left me to it with the little one in tow and I set about making my Focus shine once more.

Having seen to my bike I decided to relax with a cold beer in the front garden bathed in sunshine and relax I did. I basked in the sunshine thinking about making my rest day plural and I fear I would have done so had the hotels not already been pre-booked. A few zzzzzzzz later and the ladies returned with goodies for afternoon tea giving me time for a cuddle with Heidi before the cakes, more calories, are they trying to feed me up?

We had a marvellous Indian feast later for my birthday meal with a surprise birthday cake to follow, my favourite no less but would I have enough puff to blow the candles out?

Le JO'G	Le Tour
Rest Day 1	Rest Day 1
Box	Morzine-Avoriaz

Stage 4

Friday 30th July Pill to Kingsland

This chapter is a tale of two or even three bridges with a quick dip into south east Wales unfortunately not lasting that long.

Up in the morning after the birthday bash and thankfully no ill feelings with the curry, remember a cyclist's constitution is a delicate balance and needs to be maintained at all times. Allegedly a few years ago, poor Thor Hushovd got a shocking stomach bug and was caught on camera hurtling off his bike into the bushes more than once!

After another tremendously calorie laden breakfast we packed up and said our goodbyes, was it only 5 days since we did this? Removing and replacing the bike (already the fifth time) in the car has become a bit of a chore with having to let down the tyre, remove the front wheel and seat post then lock it to the car for safety then repeat the process at the other end, hopefully this would be my last time until home 3 days hence.

Finally we are ready and once again with sat nav set we're back to the village of Pill and the first of my three bridges, this one over the Avon. We parked in an unassuming little area close to the Avonmouth Bridge and once again removed the bike and did all the necessary modifications to get it back to being roadworthy; it gleamed in the morning sunshine, stage 4 beckoned.

Mary set off after organising the car and navigation aid, she of course, would be going a different way to get across the bridge so except for any unforeseen circumstance the next time I would see her would be in Wales, The Royal Oak in Monmouth to be exact.

I followed the cycle sign to the bridge but pretty soon got lost in downtown Pill as the signs seemed to have dried up, you wouldn't believe I could lose something that big! A kindly gent put me right and agreed the way markers for the bridge were pathetic. I set off looking forward to the ride over the river.

Through the back streets I eventually came across the cycle path that carries you over the bridge on the eastern side against the flow of traffic. It was a daunting experience with lorries thundering past at 70 mph. coming towards you but at least there was a concrete wall between us, a smaller version of the wall around the West Bank again full of graffiti but far less articulate and political.

If ever you needed real evidence of the recession you only had to look down over the bridge and see the thousands of new cars in great parking areas unsold, an amazing sight it looked like the graveyard of the twenty first century material life. Once over the bridge I dropped down into the town of Avonmouth but was soon into the dock area, not exactly an uplifting experience but what did raise the spirits, in the distance the magnificent new road bridge over the Severn came into view for the first time against the back drop of some dark clouds forming over Wales.

After contending with the usual dock traffic it was a pleasure to move away travelling north on the A4043, the wind was a kind west south westerly and was pushing me nicely to a place known as Severn Beach, unfortunately the wind did not push away the rural smells associated with the farming aspect of the area, still it was a pleasure to be back in the countryside once more.

Passing over both the M49 and the M4, which now crosses the new Severn Bridge; with the wind in my favour I made good progress and saw in the distance the old bridge still looking classy. In 1824 Thomas Telford was asked about building a bridge at this point to help speed up the mail into Wales, unfortunately nothing was constructed until 1966 when this one was opened by the Queen heralding 'the dawn of a new economic age for South Wales'.

I made my way onto this bridge by way of a cycle path, I was not disappointed with the experience of the 2 mile journey, it was breathtaking with the water far below and the new bridge shimmering in the distance like a Tea Clipper in full sail, stunning absolutely stunning. From the sublime came the ridiculous, leaving the bridge on the Welsh side it seemed I had stumbled into a Hollywood idea of what the South Bronx would look like in the 1930s. Glass and graffiti abounded on floor and wall it looked like anything but a welcome to Wales or as they say around here Croeso i Gymru, hardly a new economic dawn.

Of course the cycle signs had disappeared and I took a chance of going right, anywhere just to get back to some humanity, fortunately it was the correct choice and I eventually made it up to the main road the A466, where I spotted a proper sign welcoming drivers to Wales to hell with the cyclists!

The A466 ran on the outskirts of the lovely town of Chepstow which certainly made up for the drab beginning of the border crossing, it being quite pretty with some lovely old architecture. Beyond Chepstow I passed the famous racecourse grateful for there being no races today as there was enough traffic to contend with.

At this point on the map I remembered making a good decision when organising the route, do I go left over to the Brecon Beacons or do I carry on to go down the Wye Valley, as they say in the modern vernacular, a no brainer. I continued along the A466 to St. Arvans when miraculously the traffic seemed to melt away, must have gone to Brecon and I was left riding down a most beautiful wooded valley on an extremely quiet road next to the Wye.

Soon I reached the town of Tintern, rang a bell I thought and then I saw it, of course the Abbey or as they say around here, Abaty Tyndyrn. Now it is only a shell of a building but still looked amazing, imagine what it must have been like as a new build, I'm sure the monks would have been overjoyed to live here in these beautiful surroundings. I read somewhere that it was founded in 1131 and housed the monks of the Cistercian Order presumably until it was ransacked by good old King Henry.

It still had its uses after that though; it supposedly inspired the William Wordsworth poem "Lines Composed a Few Miles above Tintern Abbey", Alfred, Lord Tennyson's poem "Tears, Idle Tears", more than one painting by the great J. M. W. Turner and at the other end of the culture scale a band naming themselves "Tintern Abbey" certainly in the midst of lofted company but I've never heard of them or any of their songs, well I am 63.

During the planning of this ride I researched the Wye valley after finding out it was an area of outstanding beauty, I won't quarrel with that having been there. The river meandered on the border between England and Wales cutting a swathe through limestone gorges and dense woodland which teemed with wildlife and at least one bearded biker. I meandered myself enjoying the scenery then having crossed the river I rode parallel with the famous Offa's Dyke, finally reaching Monmouth or Trefynwy, for all you Welsh readers.

Over the river again and the A466 saw me ascending a not inconsequential hill but the rewards lay at the top, Mary and the pub, The Royal Oak. I thought a strange name for a pub in Wales, however, the welcome was warm along with the toasties with hand cut chips and cups of coffee, got to keep up the calories and the caffeine for the second half. Mine host turned out to be English with a few ex-pats at the bar hence The Royal Oak perhaps?

After eating our fill at the pub it was time for the next part of the journey to Kingsland a little village in northern Herefordshire. I left Mary in the car park of the pub and set off down the other side of the hill, before long I was feeling quite chilly must have been the warmth in the pub and the wind from my downhill route. I decided it was time for the gilet now never mind Scotland. I stopped and waited for my back up driver to back me up, this she duly did after flagging her down. With great ceremony I put the gilet on across my shoulders, I felt a million francs who could catch me now in the Tour, what a stunner I looked. As I hit the flat road after the hill my pace slowed and the magic of the gilet disappeared, I was now in Herefordshire just beyond Buckholt Wood back in dear old Blighty. The route now became reminiscent of Devon and Cornwall but in a mini version. Undulations certainly but of a smaller variety and yet unlike the south west counties the hedges are smaller and you can see beyond.

The gilet became a bit too warm very quickly because of these ups and downs and the previous stunning look now turned into Superman (without the body and certainly not flying) with it unzipped flapping about behind! The scenery behind those hedges was nothing short of spectacular, I'm running out of hyperboles to describe this country. There were rolling hills in my idea of a typically English style with plenty of green fields, trees, hedges and of course the odd pylon thrown in. It was simply a pleasure to be out on the road on a bike and not enclosed in a car, how much you miss going at speed and deaf to the noises of the countryside.

The A466 road had been good company since Chepstow but now it was time to move on, or as the Bard wrote 'Parting is such sweet sorrow' and sorrow it was for we had seen such beautiful scenery together so, close to the village of King's Thorn (where do they get these names from?) just before Aconbury Hill I slid ever so gently on to the A49, a road or at least its name I know well, for it is the major road through my home town heading north.

Now I have to negotiate Hereford and having made a mess of Exeter I could only hope for better things through this county town. If you look at a map of Herefordshire you will find that it is almost circular with this city virtually at its hub, the best place for a county town I suppose. On to the problems with navigating through the city though and fortunately, at home, I produced a large scale map of Hereford expecting difficulty, wish I'd done the same for Exeter.

Moving north through the outskirts of the city I once more crossed the river Wye, my last sighting I fear on my way towards the Cathedral. This is an interesting building which dates from 1079 and contains the famous Mappa Mundi, a medieval map of the world as they saw it in the 13th century. The next left took me east onto the A4110 which once more carried me northwards, I managed to get through the city with very little trouble apart from a drop of rain, towards my stop for the night at the Corners Inn in Kingsland 15 miles or so away.

The A4110 was another magical road which took me through small villages with more strange names like the Australian sounding Bush Bank and Canon Pyon, I wondered whether there was a real Canon Pyon, I don't know but there was a Canon Pyon house near another village called King's Pyon, curiouser and curiouser. Those thoughts took me to the A44 where turning right would take me to Leominster but my aim was north so straight on I go. My original hotel was Mortimer's Cross a couple of miles further on but as I have previously said they had reneged on the deal and now I turned right to Kingsland, a slight diversion from the route, to the Corners Inn my bed for the night.

Having checked in and put my bike away, thankfully in a storeroom, we decided to go for a stroll through the small village. Kingsland turned out to be really pretty, only one road but full of Blackpool Pleasure Beach crazy cottages, leaning at all angles. It started to rain and we hurried back none too soon, my empty stomach was growling. We chose to eat at the Corners, the food was good but not inspiring, still the calories were replaced.

Another walk after dinner found us at the Angel pub much better beer, atmosphere and looking at the menu, food. However, they had a group playing later and as this would have been an assault on my ears we finished our drinks and left. A lovely night nevertheless with a friendly landlady and staff pleased to welcome visitors to the area. I felt totally relaxed as we walked back to our bed ready for the next leg, further north to Whitchurch in Shropshire.

Much has been said of the many 'veterans' riding this year's Tour de France (and of course the one on LeJo'G) and this afternoon in Reims the 'Aged Brigade' demonstrated they've got the legs to go with their years of experience at the season's biggest race. Fastest of them was Alessandro Petacchi, who turned back the clock and made the 'Youth Brigade' look slow with a sprint reminiscent of his prime.

The 36-year-old from La Spezia proved that his victory in a crash-marred first stage in Brussels, when most of the peloton was held up by incidents in the final kilometre, was no stroke of luck brought on by the lack of competition in the finale. The champagne would be flowing for Petacchi following his second stage win in this year's Tour.

Amongst those other experienced hands animating the finish of stage four were Danilo Hondo, Julian Dean and Robbie McEwen, the latter jumping out of the pack with Petacchi at the 200m mark to ambush Mark Cavendish, who was swamped when lead-out man Mark Renshaw swung off in the finale. The 'Manx Missile' lacked the speed to which fans became accustomed during last year's Tour and while his HTC-Columbia teammates pulled together well - as they usually do - in the closing kilometres of today's stage, the myriad crashes and unsettled nature of this opening week may have taken their toll on Cavendish.

Le JO'G Stage 4 2010		Le Tour Stage 4 2010
Pill - Kingsland		Cambrai - Reims
		Winner Petacchi
Distance	68.233 miles	95.938 miles
Time Cycling	5hr.00m.16s.	3hr.34m.55s.
Average Speed	13.6 mph.	26.78 mph.

Stage 5

Saturday 31st July Kingsland to Whitchurch

Another day another ride. I suppose the pro riders on the Tour would be riding on rollers for about an hour to warm up their muscles for the big start, eating all the nutritious food supplied by experts and thoroughly getting fawned over, me I went off to breakfast, cereal, poached eggs on toast and lashings of coffee. I found the poached egg route the best, go to work on one is what was said, well I had two to make sure. We were up early and the eggs did not disappoint an excellent start to what I hoped would be a wonderful day.

After breakfast I set off back to the route which is on the A4110, a small diversion only from Kingsland. Today I should end up in another county, Shropshire near the town of Whitchurch for my night's sleep. Off on the bike with a spring in my step soon to be crushed by a headwind that wouldn't let me get above 13+ mph I could simply not get going but when I stopped there seemed to be no wind blowing! What a strange place. I remembered from the previous night we had to drive about a mile or so out of the village to get a signal on our mobile phones, I started looking for blonde children.

After the first mile or so on the route I passed the Mortimer's Cross Hotel all boarded up and shuttered, it didn't look too good anyway. I changed roads just after the large village of Leintwardine whose claim to fame seems to be that its High Street is on the same line as the

Roman road Watling Street, I don't know so much about that but I was now on the B4385 going north having the Devil's own time in trying to keep a good average. I'm sure the scenery was wonderful but it was a coolish cloudy day and I was struggling. The first 20 miles or so seemed to take forever so much so I got lost on the map thinking I was further on than I was, that did not go down well. It is amazing when you are not sure where you are how you fit your surroundings to the map rather than *using* the map.

I remember this happening to a bunch of us on the Calderdale hike, the walk I mentioned earlier, having limped with blisters for the last 10 miles we decided the map was wrong and the golf course was new and that's why it wasn't shown on the map, silly but we were weary and just wanted to be home, so we came down the wrong track putting us 6 miles out of our way, a salutary lesson should have been learned, obviously not, for many years later I found myself 'limping' again with tiredness from fighting the wind on the wrong part of the map.

I had a good refreshment stop and rechecked the map, found the mistake so with greater determination I rode on and made it to the cross roads with the A488 before the town of Bishop's Castle. Perhaps it was because of this mental determination or simply coincidence, I don't know but after turning right onto this road things started to improve.

I was now on the A488 bowling along quite nicely the wind seemed no longer a problem. Once again the surrounding countryside was magnificent to see, let's hear it for Shropshire a really beautiful county. The road meandered as a river between fabulous hills but always sticking to the valley bottom and then through the wonderful sounding Hope Valley it was all downhill. After the travails of the early section of the ride it was great to cease pedalling for the most part and still be moving reasonably quickly helping my average no end.

The stop for lunch was to be at the village hall in Minsterley but having phoned Mary as to her whereabouts for I couldn't find the hall, she told me neither could she and that she was parked on the Crown and Sceptre pub car park round the corner from the approach to the village. This pub is apparently one of the oldest buildings in the village but we didn't feel like a drink so other arrangements needed to be made. Next door to the pub was a little Congregational Church and a bit of luck they were holding a coffee morning that day, not in a hall next door but actually inside the church! Mary needed a toilet stop and didn't fancy nipping into the pub so in we went for coffee and cakes.

While Mary was engaged elsewhere as it were, I got into a conversation with two old dears as to why I was dressed as a Tour rider. I explained about the journey and Mary being my chief cook and bottle washer when they started telling me about their exploits in later life which seemed to make my efforts pale into insignificance. One of the ladies, they are both into their eighties, was given some flying lessons paid for by her hubby which she said,

"It was like giving pigs cherries, I loved it."

Amazingly the other one didn't want to fly a plane but jump out of one but having talked it over with her husband she decided it might be too dangerous so went hot air ballooning instead! After the chat and having eaten my full of cake and drunk the very hot coffee I was ready for my own lunch which we took outside sat in the car. Whilst enjoying the food it started to spit with rain but nothing was going to spoil my rest or Mary's lunch.

I set off again on the A488 to Pontesbury a mile or so away and in another couple I came to the village of Lea Cross which holds the Minsterley Agricultural Show in August, we were just too early, shame for it was in a beautiful setting between the local hill called Stiperstones and the River Rea. From here it's a stones throw to Shrewsbury the county town of Shropshire or should I say Salop, the abbreviated term which is derived from the Anglo-French word Salopesberia.

I followed the road through the centre of the town travelling over the river Severn close to the district of Frankwell, the birth place of the great scientist Charles Darwin who was also educated at Shrewsbury School, I bet it was hardly your local comp! It was much easier to navigate through on the map than on the streets but helpful passers by got me in the right direction for the next town on the A528 northwards and outwards to a place called Preston Gubbals.

Shrewsbury was a wonderful market town and I must say I rather liked this route for it took me through old towns and cities which have a beauty of their own with their architecture and narrow streets equally as good as the countryside that surrounded them and its good sometimes to be mixing with the traffic and people on the streets. At a place called Harmer Hill I took a right fork to the town with a strange name, Wem. Another interesting fact about the place is that it is home to the flower, sweet pea. It was introduced to the nation by a certain nursery man by the name of Henry Eckford in 1882 and was so popular the Victorians knew the town as "Wem, where the sweet peas grow".

Straight through the town I emerged onto the B5476 that took me through lovely countryside, which was changing now to more flattish plains, towards my bed for the night at Whitchurch. Little did I know that trundling along enjoying myself of what was to follow. I made good time to a roundabout south of Whitchurch on the A41, which skirted around the town and turned left to what I hoped would be my hotel on the second roundabout on this ring road. Alas and alack it was not to be.

When I arrived at the said roundabout I checked my map again but couldn't understand why there was no hotel where I had it marked. Was I doing a Calderdale all over again? After sixty odd miles of riding you get tired not just physically but mentally also, I knew the hotel was associated with a golf course but no golf course appeared on the map at this point, I just couldn't understand. I rode around and around getting more and more worked up. I even phoned Mary for help but she informed me that it was at the roundabout the sat nav had taken her there with no trouble.

I was in despair, having cycled well for the day I was now losing lots of time over a simple map reading error what to do? I asked Mary to go to the roundabout and wait, which she did and still I could not see hide nor hair this was becoming unbelievable it was though I had slipped into a parallel universe.

In desperation I rode further to the next roundabout where at last my anxiety was allayed, there she stood my outside caterer next to the large sign for the hotel. My shoulders slumped considerably with the sigh of relief. Once again I looked at the map and only then having found the hotel did I notice I had marked it on the wrong roundabout no wonder I couldn't find it. Also at this roundabout the map showed a golf course, how could I have been so stupid?

Anyway all came good in the end and I entered the complex via a steepish hill, she kept that quiet, over the top and then trundled into the car park at about 3.30pm. I asked the receptionist where I could put my bike for safe keeping she told me to take it to the room since the golfers took their bags she saw no reason why I couldn't take my bike, I agreed whole heartedly and took her at her word. The room was excellently appointed just what I needed, looking out of the window we had a wonderful view of the golf course but more spectacularly we were above the first tee!

A quick wash and brush up and since I had arrived reasonably early, we set off into Whitchurch to find a decent pub for a meal later that evening. We were having great difficulty in completing this task until we found two lady smokers outside a local hostelry, "The Last Orders". They informed us of a super pub, their words, The White Lion in the village of Ash a few miles away. Directions were a bit ropey from them both but I reckoned we could find it after the miles of navigation we had both done already.

We found the pub later in the evening, as loosely directed by the two ladies and walked through the door to an exclamation,
"You can't come in here!"
We looked at each other rather sheepishly, Mary thinking it was a private party she said,

"We're just looking for the lounge," as we had wandered into the public bar. The landlady shepherded us through the door amidst loud laughter. We sat down, I think both of us a little embarrassed. She explained that the locals assumed it was some children coming into the bar, as they do for a dare, and were going to shake them up a bit. Apologies all round and we tucked into some good grub and copious beverages. Later we left to seek our large comfortable bed and dream of home in the morning, however, as we drifted off we were not aware of the 'drama' that was to follow!

The riders at HTC-Columbia often say that each victory they take belongs to the team and no better was this demonstrated than on Thursday's stage to Montargis. After the disappointment of Wednesday's sprint into Reims, Mark Cavendish took advantage of the perfect work done by his teammates to open his stage win account in this year's Tour.
More than usual, Cavendish savoured the embraces of HTC-Columbia staff and Erik Zabel, the six-time green jersey winner and his close advisor.
Despite the best efforts of rival teams to derail the HTC-Columbia train in the final kilometres in the Montargis suburbs, the likes of Thor Hushovd, Alessandro Petacchi, Tyler Farrar, Gerald Ciolek and Robbie McEwen couldn't get the better of Renshaw and Cavendish when it counted.

Le JO'G Stage 5 2010		Le Tour Stage 5 2010
Kingsland - Whitchurch		Epernay - Montargis
		Winner Cavendish
Distance	68.726 miles	117.188 miles
Time Cycling	4hr.40m.34s.	4hr.30m.50s.
Average Speed	14.8 mph.	25.96 mph.

Stage 6

Where shall I start today? Perhaps I should start with the wonderful night's sleep or the slightly gyppy tummy (was it nasty ale? Of course the importance of bowel movement for a cyclist as I have already mentioned was not to be taken lightly, for it can lead to problems on the road as it did for Hushovd on Le Tour and me in Scotland but more of that later), or should I talk of the excellent breakfast we had consisting of just about everything you wanted from smoked salmon downwards, with beautiful aromatic fresh coffee? No I think I will start the day a little later after breakfast because that was when the tremendous start to the day went pear shaped, a puncture.

Thoroughly satiated after breakfast and pleasantly chatting with Mary I entered the room and casually looked at the bike, it was with some pride and satisfaction I beheld the red Focus in my gaze for we had come through a lot recently until the needle scratched across the record to a halt, the back tyre was flat, a puncture.

Why is it always the back tyre? Of all the punctures I have ever suffered from I could guarantee 99% were on the rear wheel. It is the same as toast always falling butter, or jam in my case, side down. Sod's Law some people will say but there are theories as to the toast, that the side buttered is heavier and thus will fall that way and I have no doubt many more. My theory for the rear puncture goes something like this; you usually miss the offending item in the road consciously or subconsciously with the front tyre as you are looking for things but as the rear wheel does not follow in line with the front exactly, BANG! However, in my case it was more obviously a slow hiss since the tyre was inflated when I arrived or more menacingly could it have been interfered with? In the early days of the French Race for instance the riders were not above cheating their way to the top so much so they had to sleep with their bikes for fear of sabotage, even sawing halfway through others bike frames and worse had been reported!

Either way the puncture had to be mended, I suppose it could have been worse it might have happened on a rainy day in the middle of the Scottish Highlands on some bleak moorland top. Looking at it in a positive way changing a tube in the warm plush surroundings of my hotel room wasn't all that bad.

Having removed the wheel from the frame taking great care to keep my hands free of the oil from the chain I took out the inner tube from inside the tyre. I felt inside the tyre for any offending sharp object when Yeow! a hawthorn about half an inch long protruded through the rubber. I retrieved a new inner tube from my saddle bag and fitted it to the wheel, replaced the tyre and put the whole assembly back onto the frame feeling pleased with myself at the speed of repair with clean hands to boot.

Trying to inflate the tyre with my pump proved a little more difficult, the more I pumped the more it hissed back at me like an angry snake, I was getting more and more frustrated by the minute. On and off came the pump from the valve in an attempt to get a better connection, was it a faulty valve surely not.

I stripped the wheel again this time with less subtleness, oil covered my hands and a grimace covered my face. The problem was a hole where the valve met the inner tube. I was beginning to get annoyed, after all it was brand new bought for the job but could the hole be down to packing in my bag? Who knows, still I have others in the car.

So down to the car to pick up the spares from my 'bike pack', no spares, in fact no bike pack! This pack consisted of everything I might need for the ride; spare tubes, spare battery, chargers for my phone and MP3 player, chain cleaner etc. etc. I realised after a few moments thinking that I must have left them in Box after I cleaned the bike on my rest day. Although I could replace the cleaner, tubes and phone this meant no more music for the rest of the ride, dear me, was I a little cross with myself.

After a few deep breaths to calm down it was back to the room to mend the puncture and by this time the clock was ticking on, thankfully I wasn't going far on this day. Having struggled to get the patch to stick using the rubber solution (why hasn't anybody come up with a better alternative yet?) I eventually blew up the tyre and fortunately it stayed that way, but for how long?

Mentally I was a bit shot so I left the room not a happy soul but I consoled myself that it wasn't raining and home was the next stop where supplies could be bought. My mood lifted as I started off with a repaired puncture and no spare inner tube down the A49 as fast as I could in the hope I would make it home before the repair gave out, I had no confidence in the tube of rubber solution sticking to the job, thankfully the road lent itself to speed, flattish and devoid of traffic, well it was Sunday morning, at one point I was even averaging 16.5 mph!

Things were going well along the Cheshire plains when just over the River Gowy at Tiverton I saw two young men making their way up the hill from the river, it seemed slow progress so I used them as a hare to keep up my speed for the hill. As I approached them I noticed they were set up for a longish ride with maps and panniers, we exchanged greetings as I passed in my hurry for home and I continued on my way.

This head down and go riding was not for me and it was a shame I saw little of the beautiful Cheshire countryside that 'flew' past. Later having stopped for a biscuit and drinks also taking the opportunity to look at the scenery one of the riders pedalled passed greeting me once more, red rag to a bull, I quickly replaced the water bottle and set off after him. Having caught him I hit the front going hell for leather thinking I probably wouldn't see him or his mate again.

Twenty four miles or so into the ride to the south east of Runcorn the back wheel did not feel right, my heart dropped, you've guessed it calamity, the patch had come adrift. I stopped at the side of the road muttering and cursing my luck to mend the puncture yet again. However, who should come past like the truck in the film "The Duel" but the two cyclists I'd been keeping company with all morning but unlike the truck in the film, they stopped to offer me help, which I thanked them for but gratefully refused allowing them to go on their way. My faith in cyclists remained strong and their offer to help put me in a much better frame of mind, noting that not all teenagers are a worry!

This time I decided the rubber solution glue was useless and so I blitzed the dreaded patch with some superglue I carried with me for just such a moment, it felt good to see the patch immovable. Off I cycled with a wing and a prayer to get home with my bike in one piece, well my inner tube at least.

Soon I was into the town of Stretton a place I knew well from my training days and then I hit south Warrington, nearly home. I turned off the A49 in the town and made my way through familiar back roads to the west. These took me through the little village of Burtonwood, which had nothing to do with brewing beer, but during the Second World War plenty of alcohol was drunk on the largest airfield in Europe which had been transferred to the Americans from the RAF in 1942.

It was built in the surrounding fields and now it's probably one of the largest and quietest housing estates with very little traffic and very little people on show. Beyond Burtonwood was just over eight miles to home and rest in my own bed. That thought kept me going well, although I was still wary of the dreaded patch letting me down, still I managed a creditable 15 mph average overall. I suppose travelling on familiar roads helped and no rain at Burtonwood which always seemed to fall on me whenever I travelled that way previously!

Untouchable. Just 24 hours after taking his first win of this year's Tour de France, Mark Cavendish equalled the record of his sprinting mentor, Erik Zabel, and with a superb sprint in Gueugnon indicated that yesterday was no fluke for the Isle of

Man's greatest cycling export, who now has 12 Tour de France stage victories to his name.

As fans witnessed the 'real' Cavendish over the final 200 metres of yesterday's run into Montargis, the Manxman's trademark sprint was again on show - albeit with even more panache, lustre and confidence - following another brilliant dose of team work from HTC-Columbia throughout the day's 227.5km parcours.

With a commanding winning margin of two bike lengths, Cavendish celebrated with contented pleasure after the finish, yesterday's drought breaker giving him the confidence needed to get back on track despite a less-than-ideal start to this year's Tour.

Le JO'G Stage 6 2010		Le Tour Stage 6 2010
Whitchurch - Home		Montargis - Gueugnon
		Winner Cavendish
Distance	45.962 miles	142.188 miles
Time Cycling	3hr.05m.12s.	5hr.37m.42s.
Average Speed	15.0 mph.	25.26 mph.

Rest Day 2

Monday 2nd August Home

Having arrived home yesterday in the early afternoon it was good to just chill out with a cup of tea and accept the praise from the neighbours. I felt good, really good but I didn't get ahead of myself I still had eight more days to go, the second week, some races remember are won in the second week, how would I fare?

Today after a relaxing night I awoke and felt everything was right with the world, down for breakfast and this time just porridge and toast, hang the calories for a day. After the early morning food I unpacked my belongings for my outside caterer turned wash maid and realised there was a map book missing, my map book with the A4 sheets which I enclose in the wallet and strap to my handlebars.

Oh Calamity! I sat and thought when did I last see it? Of course, it was in the room in the last hotel on the chest of drawers next to the television waiting to be picked up and packed away but picked up it was not never mind packed away. Memory, hither come; William Blake knew exactly what I was going through. What a morning I had yesterday, one I hope never to be repeated.

I phoned the hotel and eventually spoke to the receptionist about a book of maps left in room 303 (at least I remembered the room number), it took me an age to spell out what I meant by a book of maps and then she transferred me to Housekeeping, my head dropped. When I finally managed to explain to them the nature of the book, she said,

"With a red cover?"

"Yes," I replied.

"We have it here."

I felt like J.R. Hartley trying to find his book on Fly-fishing.

Eventually we were together with this little problem and she suggested posting it on but obviously it would not have arrived before I set off for Scotland the following day or probably the following week knowing the Royal Mail. However, I accepted the offer and decided other arrangements for duplicate maps had to be made, still nice to be home and sleeping in my own bed, keep thinking those happy thoughts.

My other arrangements for the maps turned out to be using Mary's book and printing the extra large scale ones for when they were needed. Plenty of washing took place turning our home into a Chinese Laundry and of course there was time for us to replenish parts even beers don't reach. It was good to see younger son Robert, his wife Lisa and grandson Ricardo who gave me great words of support and encouragement for the journey yet to come, could he be a budding Cavendish? I think more likely a budding Messi.

The bike was due for another clean even though it had let me down in Shropshire, talking of which the rear tyre was still well inflated so I left the inner tube on the wheel for the time being. I had to go and purchase more inner tubes of course to replace the ones left down in Box and more chain oil etc. I then hunted out my old mobile phone and charger to replace the one I had since its charger was also left down in Wiltshire along with my MP3 player's charger, pity I couldn't hunt out my old MP3 player as well (haven't got one that's why) ah well I'll just have to whistle a happy tune whenever I feel alone in the wilds of Scotland.

At the end of the rest day we were both well organised again and couldn't wait for the following day, the next leg in the company of cycling friends George and Haydn, with of course their wives, (how else would they get home?)

Le JO'G   Le Tour

Rest Day 2   Rest Day 2

Home   Pau

Stage 7

Tuesday 3rd August Home to Oxenholme

Oxenholme here we come, George and Haydn ride today as my domestiques. We were up early for breakfast and then packed the suitcases, from now on I had no rest days so cycling clothes had to be used on a rota basis, hoping they didn't become too smelly!

The sun shone as we ate and I remember thinking at least it won't rain today the forecast being for sun and cloud. The rest of the forecasts for the journey, from Metcheck, were filed away to be used later. I was excited to be riding with company especially my two training friends it would make for good variety on the journey since now I had no MP3 player.

George was notorious for being an early riser and I do mean early, he walked his dog at obscene times in the morning having been stopped by the police on more than one occasion mistaking him for a burglar. His wife, Irene had a heck of a time from keeping him away from my house, he had been up since five o'clock or so champing at the bit, or should that be handlebars, they arrived 30 minutes earlier than agreed, time for a brew.

Haydn arrived not long after giving us a pessimistic weather view of showers according to today's radio weather, so my domestiques both dressed for the occasion, I decided to remain optimistic and brave the conditions was that hardy or foolhardy?

I live down a typical farmer's lane lined with hawthorn hedges so riding a bike along here was asking for trouble and that, none of us wanted, so the first part of the journey was spent walking to the main road looking out for the dreaded thorns on the floor. At the top of the lane I checked my cycle computer and realised that I had not entered the results from the previous stage into my log (my memory again!) so I rode back to the house and back up the lane (to hell with the punctures) to start off at the later time of 9.30am considering the early start to the day with my domestiques.

The birthday book which Mary bought me shows the route actually going past the top of my lane and so now at the moment we are following in their tyre tracks on our way to Appley Bridge our first drinks stop. In the book it says there is a long pull up to the town from the Leeds and Liverpool canal in the valley bottom, it is not wrong. These roads I travel with my bike frequently and know them very well but the hills do not get any easier for all that. Out of breath at the first stop it seemed my domestiques had overestimated my fitness and strength I needed to rein them back in if I was to reach Oxenholme in one piece.

The country lanes from here were quiet and free of traffic ideal for cycling and we made good progress towards Preston passing Wymott prison but this time I preferred to cycle than be an inmate. The prison lied just to the west of the town of Leyland which of course had been synonymous with the name Leyland Trucks for many many years involving local jobs and even people from my home town, my best man served his apprenticeship there when he was younger.

On roads I knew, we had no trouble getting to the outskirts of Preston at the Riversway Docklands when it all fell apart. I had previously checked the CTC route which takes you on the A49 through the centre of Preston full of traffic and right turn problems on big roads. I amended that by going the way into Preston which I used all the time hence we were around the Docklands area which was quite pleasant.

From here it was a mere hop skip and a jump to get to the B6241 to take us back into the countryside north of the city, in theory. For this reason I did not have a map of this area knowing it like the back of my hand as I did, pride certainly went before a fall. I took a wrong turn and suddenly we were lost around the back streets of Preston goodness knows where, we cycled and cycled around and around seeing nobody who could help and then it started to rain. I pulled up outside a Taxi office and went in to ask, somehow we were on the correct road but coming from the totally opposite direction, all's well that ends well I suppose but my standing in front of my domestiques took a pasting.

Soon we were flying north through the town and the villages of Ingol and Woodplumpton thanks to my pacemen and from here across country, a route I had previously checked and this time no problem, to our next stop en-route a large hostelry by the Lancaster canal in the village of Bilsborrow. The rain by now was teeming down making things a little difficult for us but we had to steel ourselves and get from under the shelter and move on following the original CTC route along the A6 to Garstang, our lunch stop with the ladies and John, Haydn's son.

The quietness of the countryside gave way to the hustle and bustle of a major highway now coming from Luton to finish in Carlisle but originally it began with the A1 from the London Borough of Barnet. We managed the two miles to the turn off to Garstang easily enough and entered once again rural tranquility up to the pub, The Wheatsheaf for lunch. By the time we reached the car park we were wet through and in need of a hot meal, I was anyway.

The wives were inside enjoying coffee and hot chocolate well at least two were, Linzi, Haydn's other half was shopping somewhere and turned up later. We parked our bikes under the cover of the smoker's corner amidst billows of cigarette smoke coming from a gent who would keep regaling us with his incessant chat when all we wanted was to go indoors to get warm. Finally we made it into the pub to be greeted by the ladies as men home from the Front; I rather liked all this adulation as wet and as cold as we were, it warmed the cockles of my heart.

After ordering hot drinks, cold beer did not seem to be on the menu, we bored our back up girls with talk about the ride throughout the morning but hunger began to get the better of us and food needed to be eaten. Eventually various lunches were ordered and thinking of all the carbs I would need later I chose Chilli chips topped with mushy peas, funnily enough neither of my domestiques wanted to be behind me in the afternoon, I couldn't think why?

After the meal I felt less like going for a bike ride than going to the guillotine, a good sleep seemed a better option perhaps it was the extra helping of mushy peas. At last we dragged ourselves away from the good company trying hard not to give in to the evil thoughts of having a few pints packing the bikes in the cars and driving to Oxenholme. We started off again and made our way back to the A6 to travel the trunk road to Lancaster, by now the rain had abated and the sun was trying to break the strangle hold the clouds seemed to have had on the sky.

My domestiques were doing me proud, we kept up a good pace along this busy road keeping parallel with the M6 and the West Coast Main Line. We came to the village of Galgate (apparently pronounced Golget!) two miles or so south of the city of Lancaster, passing through this village seemed to be the thing to do on this journey of mine since the name Galgate in Old English means 'the road to Scotland'. A popular opinion amongst locals however, would have the name shortened from Gallows Gate being the last village condemned people would pass through on the way to their place of execution, presumably at Lancaster Gaol, I prefer the road to Scotland thank you very much!

Lancaster, I was told is full of one way streets making life difficult for the stranger in a car so I was not looking forward to navigating our way through the city but my theory of passing through cities on large roads proved a winner this time. As it turned out it was a bit of a breeze simply following the signs for the A6 at least it was for Haydn and George, it seemed I just followed on behind shouting the wrong directions!

After we crossed the River Lune we were heading north again with Morecambe to the west, we resisted the urged to visit, though the temptation was not great and moved onto our next village with the grand sounding name of Bolton-Le-Sands, have we moved on to 'Le Tour'? Apparently it was given the prefix of Sands to differentiate it from the other Bolton near Manchester as both were on the same railway line.

Beyond Bolton came the town of Carnforth, of course everyone knows its claim to fame, the railway station being used in the magnificent film Brief Encounter. It was known to me and both my outriders for a very different and much more painful reason. Many years ago we set off on a long distance walk from Carnforth that used no imagination of the surrounding countryside.

It involved tramping the streets and canal side by the noisy A6 and two loops of the famous town. Susceptible to blisters the hard roads and pavements did little to help, Haydn and I were not happy as you can imagine, we were literally walking on water as they burst one by one. The final insult came as we were directed to walk along the seashore after walking the streets, over salt marshes which meant having to jump across wide deep rivulets.

That was the last straw both Haydn and myself decided that discretion was the better part of valour and went to the pub to lick our wounds, metaphorically speaking of course. George who did not know the meaning of blisters continued with the rest of the group as tired as he was to complete the distance, good for him but I think we may have made the wiser choice, the beer was good.

Leaving the bad memories of Carnforth behind we moved to an area George knew and loved very well, Yealand Conyers but unfortunately we had to move away from the A6 to the A6070 towards Cumbria and Burton-in-Kendal a fine little village but not today, we picked the day when road re-surfacing was in progress and it was virtually closed. We were still travelling quite quickly beyond Burton-in-Kendal thanks to Haydn at the front, who had trained for this stage quite religiously, when unfortunately George's calf started to give him some gyp, an old tennis wound that erupted after sustained exercise, what with Haydn's burst of speed I was thankful for George's injury to be slowing down and grateful I could now begin to admire the South Lakeland scenery.

Admire it we all did for the views of fells, crags and simply green fields were wonderful to behold in this South Lakeland enclave. It is amazing to me how many people zoom past here on the motorway up to the Lake District with its high fells and touristy places when behind them is the peace and quiet of a typical English countryside, more fool them.

Through the village of Endmoor and George was now riding through gritted teeth trying to keep a smile on his face, I told him that there were only 3 miles to go to the pub, just think of the beer, I'm afraid it had little effect on his leg but his taste buds picked up. Of all the times for it to happen but somehow I missed the turn off for Oxenholme and struggled to find out where we were on the map at least it gave us a rest although I'm sure George just wanted to plough on.

At last I found the mistake and turned off the main road to the famous Oxenholme station where countless trains fly through here going north, south and of course the gateway branch line to the Lakes. Strangely enough history showed there seemed to have been more murders at the station than a Midsomer episode but probably its best claim to fame was being used by

Arthur Ransome in his book series Swallows and Amazons, its fictional name then being Strickland Junction.

We ended up at the station confronted by a very large hill; we stopped to check the map. I was convinced The Station pub my stop for the night was indeed up the hill but my compatriots were not having any of that, they wanted to ask the fellow stood at the bus stop part way up the hill to be sure. I was duly dispatched, unluckily for us the man was of Asian origin and spoke very little to no English.

Every time I asked him for directions to the Station pub I was confronted with him replying, station, station and pointing down the hill to the railway station. I tried to get across it was the pub I wanted but only station was the reply. It reminded me of the sketch in Only Fools and Horses where the unfortunate Frenchman who was accidently kidnapped in the back of Del boy's truck could only say Gary, Gary!

I cut my losses and decided to ask a couple who had just started to walk up the hill, my worst fear was proved correct.

"Up the hill," I shouted to my dejected domestiques.

Up the hill we went to be met by the ladies and John stood in the car park. We riders decided to get changed in the room into some dry clothes and perhaps a hot shower but unfortunately no hot water for showers (water only heated up at 5 o'clock!) the cold shower was not exactly an ice bath and did nothing for my circulation still we ended up in dry clothes all red faced ready for a few drinks.

We then had a scrumptious meal and then more beers. By now these were taking their toll for we were getting tired. The girls organised their sat navs and soon they were all leaving for home whilst me and Mary would be on our way to Bonny Scotland the next day - Och Aye dunoo! It had been a memorable day for all of us but now we were both ready for bed, to dream about Shap and the next stage.

Sylvain Chavanel (Quick Step) won his second stage of this year's Tour de France at Station des Rousses on Saturday, and completed another double, taking over the yellow jersey, just as he also did in Spa at the end of stage 2.
Unlike in Spa, however, the history books will show no asterisk against Chavanel's name after this victory – which, again,he achieved alone.
If his win in Spa carried a hollow ring, with the race neutralised behind him following the crash-marred descent of the Stockeu, at the summit of Station des Rousses, there was only acclaim and admiration after a gutsy and perfectly-timed and executed counterattack.
From Chavanel himself, there was an exuberant, fist-pumping, medallion-kissing celebration along the finishing straight, while, behind him, there were skirmishes and a minor sort out of the overall contenders, but no significant winners or losers.

Le JO'G Stage 7 2010		Le Tour Stage 7 2010
Home - Oxenholme		Tournus - Station des Rousses
		Winner Chavanel
Distance	68.321 miles	103.438 miles
Time Cycling	4hr.25m.08s.	4hr.22m.52s.
Average Speed	14.8 mph.	23.61 mph.

Stage 8

Wednesday 4th August Oxenholme to Cummertrees

Since starting this journey I have ridden just short of 500 miles and not once have I moaned about the weather especially the wind, oh I have talked about it but not as yet complained. Well I am now bellyaching, the wind, instead of the prevailing south westerly, expected in summer it was a north westerly veering to west north west gusting at 25+ mph no less. This was not good for any cyclist weighing about 10 stone wet through, with it blowing in his face when he was attempting to cycle 73 miles to Scotland and I was that poor cyclist.

Sorry for the whinge but I just felt I needed to get that off my chest for it was a very difficult day of cycling especially in the latter half after lunch as reflected in my very low average of 13 mph, although I do appreciate it was my first 'mountain' stage, the 'mountain' in question, Shap Fell.

As a young cyclist, there were two hills that sent shivers down the back of any youngster in my day, not that we could ever get near them never mind attempt them; the Cat and Fiddle in Derbyshire and Shap Fell in Westmorland now Cumbria. Since I knew I was going over Shap I decided to discover a few things about it. I came across a website written by Malcolm Stubbs that said it all.

In the days before the building of the M6, pre 1971, vehicle drivers heading to Scotland were forced to negotiate the treacherous climes of the A6 over Shap Fell where they could experience all types of weather. This route was long-feared by lorry drivers passing between England and Scotland because of the devilishly long climb (and descent when coming home). There are a number of vicious bends and this was and still is a legendary piece of road to many. They nicknamed the area "The Jungle", and the infamous Jungle Cafe was founded there in the 1930s.

To commemorate these epic journeys a monument was erected at the highest point of the route of the A6 over the fell. A sad end to this tale is that the Jungle Cafe has now long gone and the site has become home to Kendal Caravans. Now you can see as a child listening to these stories how it became embedded into cycling folklore and why today I was a little concerned about the fell. Now for the ride.......

Awakening a little later than anticipated, probably the beer from the night before, I attempted a wash, plenty of hot water this time but now no cold due to a mains water leak further down the pipeline. They certainly have their water issues around here, anyway that wasn't my problem I had other worries. After breakfast I eked out my water reserves from the previous day to my bottles before setting off at 9 o'clock instead of the original time of 8.30, I seem to be taking longer and longer to get ready.

I freewheeled down the uphill of yesterday into the town of Kendal known as the Gateway to the Lakes and also famous for its world renowned Mint Cake. I survived its myriad of one way streets and emerged into 'daylight' on the A6 to an ominous sign:

SHAP FELL 1400ft DANGEROUS IN WINTER

The dread of the early tales returned, the arrow painted on the road pointing the way to SHAP simply reinforced my destiny. At this point, the road appeared to rise or was my mind playing tricks? Another mile and it certainly did rise and quite sharply taking my breath away, this ascent went on for about a mile and suddenly it was as though I was in a plane overlooking the town nestling in the valley.

Onward I went, feeling like Indurain grinding out the miles (yes, miles) on Alpe d'Huez but again probably looked more like poor Tommy on Ventoux on that fateful day in '67. Seven miles it carried on my legs tiring more and more. The views, however, were gorgeous, tarmac and more tarmac!

The road continued its upward trend until a mile past the hamlet of Watchgate gave me a little respite on a flattish part of the route time for a drink. Once more I headed upward to a pass between two fells both over 1500 feet high, with the mist ominously descending I came over the top and thankfully a downward freewheel to Borrow Beck, a small stream, breathed life back into my heart and lungs.

From the Beck I could see the summit over a mile away rising up to 1400 feet. Slowly and slowly I reached close to the summit with some roadwork's traffic lights in my way I was hoping for green to keep powering on but curses they were on stop so I had to rest awhile. As I took a breather I watched cyclists coming the other way, flying down,

"Just you wait," I said to myself, "it will be my turn in a short while" thinking of the other side.

Near the top I spied Mary, with the dark clouds gathering behind her, what a welcome sight she was.

Over the top I went hoping to emulate the flying cyclists from the other side, not to be, the rain had started to fall and the wind from the NW was blowing up a storm! All the way down the fell and into Shap village itself I had to pedal like a sprinter for the line just to keep going against the wind and the rain, upset was not the word.

Through the village, quite a pleasant place although it would have been much better in some summer sunshine I followed the A6, the road I had been travelling since Garstang the previous day. There was a definite absence of traffic on this road since Garstang, it was becoming more like a bye-way, I dare say the M6 motorway has had a big say in its decline as a trunk road, good for me, however.

The rain began to peter out to a spit as I criss crossed the M6 and the railway line on my way to the large market town of Penrith about nine miles away. This town was once part of the old county of Cumberland and due to its strategic position on the route to Scotland, since Roman times it had developed as a military centre. My observations of Penrith were the hilly roads, apart from it being a beautiful town, but simple enough to get through on my trek for lunch at the Stoney Beck pub a couple of miles away.

When I arrived there Mary was nowhere to be seen, a quick phone call found her at an Equestrian Centre up the lane before the pub unfortunately having the same post code. Finally we got it sorted and met outside the Stoney Beck which was an up market Bistro, not a great pub to have lunch in the car park and then a quick visit to the toilet so we made our way up the road a couple of miles to the small village of Plumpton and enjoyed another wonderful potpourri of food from Mary with excellent coffee.

After the great lunch the 'dessert' was certainly pear-shaped! I set off in good spirits but was soon put in my place by the gale in my face. I read a quote by Lance Armstrong in his autobiography: "Cycling is so hard, the suffering is so intense, that it's absolutely cleansing," well I can tell you honestly I did not feel cleansed in any way shape or form battling through the headwind, although I did suffer intensely in trying to reach 13+ mph. with my little legs getting more and more tired on my way to Carlisle, the county town of Cumbria. It was 11 miles of sheer brutality against the gusting nor'wester in open country before I made the south of the Border city, nicknamed so because of its close proximity to Scotland, with its wind protection amongst the buildings.

In the city I found most of the cycle lane surface had been ripped up obviously to be redone at a later date, that later date had not yet arrived and it was very difficult to keep my balance lurching through potholes and unstable road surface. For safety's sake I moved away from the cycle lane to the carriageway whereupon I had an altercation with a young lady driver in a Vauxhall Corsa, backed up with her companion in the passenger seat, complaining that she had nearly run me over. I was not happy, you can imagine.

The argument lasted a few hundred yards or so about who should be where on the road when we had to part company by the Cathedral, she to go straight on and me to turn right to follow the A7 over the River Eden and through where Hadrian's Wall stood many years ago.

On the A7 now I moved north through the suburb of Kingstown in very dense traffic and in the wrong lane, I blame the road markings, it did not go down well with the locals and I kept my head down trying not to hear what they were saying! Away from the city now and the road surface continued to be not especially good for cyclists very uneven and with the wind still blowing it was very difficult for me to get any kind of speed and I was becoming more and more weary and not a little cold, still Scotland beckoned but first to Longtown closer to the border.

Following the extremely straight A7, from Carlisle to Longtown I was obviously riding on a Roman Road and it seemed to be going on forever, straight roads against wind was not exciting for this cyclist. After a good three quarters of an hour to do the six miles I was glad to reach the town and after crossing the River Esk it was a novelty just to move my handlebars to the left on the A6071 to Gretna and the border.

Another 3 miles saw me crossing the M6 and after turning right over the River Sark I was at last in Bonny Scotland but it looked less bonny at the moment, the tacky sign reinforcing my thoughts. Further on I came of course to the First and Last House Marriage Room with a Chinese couple posing for a photograph, was it a wedding shot or just the proverbial snap, either way stopping wasn't an option to offer congratulations, I may never have started again.

"Go west young man" was a paraphrase used by Horace Greely of the New York Tribune in 1865, taking him at his word it is exactly what I did on my bike in 2010. However, remember at the beginning of this day I said I was unlucky with the wind, its force and direction, then you have a picture of what the next 11 miles going west was like. I think tiredness got the better of me eventually and I just succumbed to the wind, I was going ever slower, a cycling pal would have been a godsend now but it wasn't to be.

I was pedalling on the B721 which also doubled as the National Cycle Route 74 from the little hamlet of Rigg. Route 74 is 44 miles long and connects Route 7 to south Lanarkshire, was I glad I was only riding 7 miles of those 44 today. For all the moaning I've done and I know I've done some, I have to say it was a lovely quiet road shadowing as it did the railway line from Gretna to Dumfries and beyond and to boldly go is what I did, towards Annan.

This was a less than charming town full of red sandstone buildings but now blackened by years of pollution, there were two saving graces however; one, the wonderful war memorial and two, the three arched bridge over the River Annan, designed by Robert Stevenson, the Scottish civil engineer of lighthouse fame not to be confused with the other Robert Stephenson the English engineer who designed the steam locomotive, the Rocket.

There was a magnificent sight as I crossed the three arched bridge, a couple of salmon fishermen plying their craft on the meandering river in the afternoon sunlight, it almost made the efforts of the last five hours or so worth it, a great picture to keep in my mind to the end of the journey.

Through the town and I was 3 miles from my bed at the Solway Sporting Breaks in the village of Cummertrees but they seemed the longest 3 miles I had ever done. At last there was Mary to greet me, my journey had ended, after putting away the bike in the garage around the back I collapsed into a chair in our room, boy did I need that recovery drink!

After a shower I was ready for food but Annan was a veritable desert of pubs, restaurants or cafes. This was nothing more than I expected having seen the town earlier or perhaps we were not looking in the right places. We were told of the Golf Club at Powfoot serving meals, so hotfoot we drove round there and a splendid view across the Solway Firth met our eyes, we were smitten.

Inside we ordered food twice, the first two being off in true Basil Fawlty style but third time lucky we were served with an excellent meal, coupled with the beer it certainly hit the spot. It was a most beautiful view looking out of the window across the Firth to the northern fells of the Lakes and with the sun now shining across the sky it certainly made up for the wind and the rain of the day, peace at last.

There were two defining images of the eighth stage of the Tour de France. One saw a battered, bruised and decidedly ragged Lance Armstrong, shepherded by his RadioShack teammate Jani Brajkovic, struggling across the line at Morzine-Avoriaz, almost 12 minutes down.

The other saw Andy Schleck (Saxo Bank) come of age with a stunning stage win. And it was this second image that should prove more significant in the coming days, since it suggested a shift in the balance of power, from the defending champion and favourite, Alberto Contador (Astana), towards last year's runner-up. While the story of last year's Tour was of Schleck being unable to respond to Contador's repeated accelerations in the mountains, here it was the other way around.

An elite, 13-man group had just passed under the one-kilometre-to-go kite when the Luxembourg rider made his one, decisive move. Contador, whose Astana teammate Daniel Navarro had led almost the entire way up the 13.6km mountain, reacted quickly to his rival's attack, sprinting after his rear wheel, but he couldn't close the gap.

Indeed, the race was on, prompting Samuel Sanchez (Euskaltel-Euskadi) to pounce after Schleck. Approaching the line, with the Olympic champion having joined Schleck in front, it was Sanchez who led it out and looked as though he had it, but Schleck came around him, glancing across at his rival as he drew level, and then inching ahead to claim his first ever stage win in his third Tour.

Le JO'G Stage 8 2010		Le Tour Stage 8 2010
Oxenholme – Cummertrees		Station des Rousses–
		Morzine-Avoriaz
		Winner Schleck
Distance	73.521 miles	118.125 miles
Time Cycling	5hr.42m.59s.	4hr.54m.11s.
Average Speed	13.0 mph.	24.09 mph.

Stage 9

Thursday 5th August Cummertrees to Stair

This was a three section day as opposed to the normal two sections; before lunch then after lunch Up to now breakfasts have not been much to write home about in the excitement stakes, not to say I didn't have wonderful discourse with my lady back up driver over the toast but there were carbs and I ate them, but today I felt the mealtime needed a piece written for itself.

Once again with regard to the food this morning, good but unexciting however the conversation was much more interesting. As there was only one table in the dining room we shared it with two fishermen from London, who have been travelling up to Annan for years to fish the river, was it them I saw the other day?

The talk we had with the two Londoners was fascinating about the town of Annan, they could certainly give Wikipedia a run for its money but then again like the website was everything true? They regaled us over breakfast about the history of Annan, they, as I said have been coming up here a few years and have got to know a few things I was wondering whether he was going to tap his nose after that! Perhaps he should have, when I heard the tale.

Allegedly, the town was commandeered by the government around the First World War to become an armaments and explosive manufacturing town along with Gretna down the road, which it remained until the

1970s. The town believe it or not was then sold off to the highest bidder! A Mr. Gordon Clarke, the local 'Mafia Don' won the auction and it became his fiefdom, well some of it anyway. From then on the town became more and more downtrodden; I suppose his behaviour was a bit like the despots of the modern world. Now, not wanting a libel suit hanging around my neck I checked this information on the Wikipedia website and others and no mention was there of a Mr. G. Clarke or Clark who had done this dastardly deed.

The armaments factory was true in as much as there was a munitions building at Eastriggs between Gretna and Annan which was served mainly by the good ladies of the two towns. So whatever the truth of it, the conversation passed a very interesting breakfast, but unfortunately I had to leave and get on the road to the tiny village of Stair in south Ayrshire my next stop for the night.

After that illuminating breakfast I got on my bike and said my goodbyes to Mary, to see her once again for lunch at a place called Moniaive and looking at the map, it was in the middle of nowhere. I set off on the trek and spied my first road kill of the journey so far, Reynard the Fox who met an untimely death last night (for it still looked fresh if you pardon the expression) presumably by colliding with some vehicle.

I was amazed really to have seen so few deaths on the road in all the miles I have travelled, apart from the insect life, beetles and the like but I can't count them as road kill surely. One measly fox, still I'm sure the inhabitants of Watership Down were pleased; plenty of bunnies would have slept sounder in their burrows that night.

Once again I am tracking the railway northwest to Dumfries on rather a pleasant road with, at the moment, little wind to hinder my progress, life is pleasant in the first section of my ride. However, I must talk about Dumfries for I have been before believe it or not forty odd years ago camping with friends just south of the town by the river Nith.

A dog walker used to call for a chat and a brew every morning and it was he who informed us that the Dumfries football team was called the Queen of the South. I had often wondered, as a boy, where or who was this Queen of the South seen many times on the television programme Grandstand with the ticker tape machine giving out the football scores on a late Saturday afternoon, now I knew.

The wonderful road I was on joined the very busy A75, which unfortunately I had to travel on for five miles before turning onto a 'less busy' road but everything is relative, it was a bit like out of the fire and into the frying pan! Fortunately there was an alternative route as supplied by the CTC in a couple of miles just beyond the northwest suburbs of Dumfries, on the B729, I couldn't wait. The noise of the traffic was left far behind as I wound myself around the bends of this peacefully quiet road.

The pleasure was short lived, however, as the wind and the road picked up! The wind was now in my face again but I'm not complaining and the road took an upward turn for about 5 miles, yes I counted every one going from 30 to 540 feet in height. If I closed my eyes, apart from losing my balance, I felt I was on the Col du Tourmalet with Lance oh the joy!

Finally I reached the top exhilarated and thirsty for a drink so I stopped to admire the view and what scenery there was, surrounded by hills and fells with woods and streams and silence. From the top the way down was just as slow battling against the wind, it was all I could do to reach 14+ mph. downhill!

Moving on, the wonderful countryside kept my pecker up as I passed through the sleepy village of Dunscore, in fact it was more like the dead village of Dunscore; everything was closed. Riding along the valley next to Cairn Water, a meandering river, with the sun shining was another breathless experience, the breathlessness coming from both the scenery and pedalling in equal parts. I was well on track for lunch and I couldn't wait, phoning Mary she told me the pub stop, the Craigdarrach Arms was closed so she had found a village car park were we could eat.

Riding through the village more bunting on display as in Gunnislake, surely they have found out I'm passing through, it can't be a coincidence, can it? I sat down to my lunch in the sunshine by the river Dalwhat Water and ate it with relish, once again a truly delicious selection of goodies; tuna, mixed bean salad, cous cous, banana sandwiches and hot coffee what more could a hungry cyclist want?

And so begins the second part of my story. After lunch was finished I set off in full heart over the river through the village and out into open country again. From the valley bottom the road ascended with some venom in places with a constant winding upwards, the starting point being about 100 feet above sea level rising to 1000 feet at the pass 5 miles further on! This however, seemed wilder than the previous stretch, more craggy and rocky with occasional Forestry Commission woods mostly cut down leaving no windbreak, so with fern and heather for company I set myself against the wind, as ever from the west blowing into my face and gusting stronger. Towards the top after toiling uphill, unlike the great climber Pantani, I was being blown about by the wind like a kite on a piece of string as the road opened up onto really rugged countryside.

A drizzle had started to fall and in my attempt to don my rain jacket the westerly ripped at the cagoule as I struggled to put my arms through the sleeves, I was cold and miserable the mist was descending around me like a cloak of invisibility. I felt lost and alone, the total lack of any signal on my mobile and any vehicle from a tractor to a Porsche, on this road had me worried, I was thinking you just don't want to fall off your bike and break a leg here or it would be a skeleton they'd find!

The marathon runners say they hit a 'wall' when they lose all energy because of tiredness, lack of fluids or hunger and can no longer go on. Many years ago in the Empire Games of 1954, before they became known as the Commonwealth Games, Jim Peters, a marathon runner of some note, had set 4 world records in the previous 2 years but fell repeatedly in sight of the line from exhaustion after opening up a lead of 20 minutes to his nearest rival. He had run the entire marathon on a scorching hot day without drinking any water and ended up crawling to the line but never making it.

At that moment on the top of the fell all alone I probably felt as low as Jim Peters did all those years ago, not through any dehydration but with a feeling of loneliness, weariness and just sick of being buffeted by the wind and now the rain and of course would I make it? Mentally I had 'bonked' in the American vernacular.

Haydn, my biker friend once bonked on the top of Hellvellyn in the Lake District during a long distance walk. He was dehydrated and tired and was having an altercation with a walk marshal over his drink, Haydn wanted it and the marshal was trying to save some for other people, at the time I thought the confrontation could have turned nasty so the only way was to get him down from the cold and the wind howling around him, this I did and thankfully he revived in the valley bottom.

That is exactly what I needed to do as well, get down as quickly as I could to some semblance of normality away from the wind and hopefully the rain. It was at this point I realised, a defining moment of the trip, that if the wind doesn't change its direction then I would have to modify my expectations of averaging 14 to 15 mph in the day and concentrate on 13 to 14, if I didn't then I don't think my legs would be attached to my body at John O'Groats! It was another low time for me and a disappointment in my speed.

Off the top I went pedalling hard against the elements but the rain thankfully was abating. After a lot of effort I made it to the bottom and not only did the rain stop but the wind was far less a problem, although the next hill was. It rose to about 1000 feet over the next six miles but I felt better although not any quicker. I rolled up my sleeves and started the grind upwards. The scenery was much less bleak and my outlook brightened considerably.

After 4 miles I found myself on a long straight drag to the top and the rain came back in buckets, my bright disposition disappeared down the drain with the rainwater. Nearing the top by the side of Loch Muck, I kid you not, I passed over a hairy caterpillar, moth or butterfly to be I don't know, it had crawled the width of a very wide road and was nearly to the other side when my front wheel just missed it. I thought of the courage the caterpillar had shown to make the journey and vowed to complete my trek in recognition of its bravery, that is if my back wheel didn't get it, remember what I said about back wheel punctures, I told you I had bonked mentally.

Over the top of the hill and down into the town of Dalmellington I decided to stop for refreshments. The sun broke through the rain clouds to warm and dry me (must have missed the hairy one, thank you God) so I divested my rain jacket wrapped it up in its bag and in what was now becoming heat I rode into the third section.

After Dalmellington the road surface became smoother and flat so I was able to gather up a bit of speed, all relative you realise. The next town on the route was Patna which appeared on my left atop of a hill looking for all the world like a government owned town where most if not all the houses I could see had the same council house look, very strange to see. It was originally built by William Fullerton in 1802 to provide housing for workers in the coal fields of his estate but I'm sure these weren't they, although the ones I could see could have been built by his ancestors they were all so alike.

I stopped to check the map and suddenly a car coming the opposite way slammed on its brakes bringing the vehicle to a screeching stop. The driver wound down his window and looked across the road at me, at this point I wondered what strange Scottish bye-law I had broken,

"Can I help ye, are ye lost?" he shouted.

Relieved I called back,

"No thanks I'm fine."

Then I noticed the bike on a rack at the back of the car, wonderful the cyclists of Britain forever helpful, unlike the French policeman on stage 14 of the 1988 tour when he sent the leader the wrong way with 300metres to go and allowed Italy's Massimo Ghirotto, who hadn't a hope of winning, to cross the line first with Scotland's Robert Millar second.

After Patna the route took me right onto the B730 which went northeastwards thus placing the irritable wind behind and at the side of me. From here it was 9 miles of bike heaven again, the sun on my back and a fair wind to carry me home. The roads were reasonably flattish and I made good time to Stair, a very drawn out village, for my stop at the aptly named Stair Inn.

This was a wonderful pub with a decent room for the night although there was a notice about the dreaded midges, our first encounter:

DO NOT OPEN THE WINDOW AT NIGHT

We had an excellent meal in the evening, I certainly ate my fill and since there was nothing else in the village and the wee beasties were about we stayed for a couple of pints in the bar and a chat to the locals.

At some time during the night however, we were awakened from our deep slumber, at least mine was, by an alarm. Not thinking it was a fire alarm since there was no shouting I peered out of the window with bleary eyes and spied my car on its own with no warning lights flashing, so back I went to sleep when the din had finally died down.

This year's Tour de France has been a good vintage for French riders; two stage wins and the maillot jaune for Sylvain Chavanel have made it memorable for the local fans, who were treated to more home grown success with a stage win for Française des Jeux's Sandy Casar in Saint-Jean-de-Maurienne after another interesting day in the Alps.

The day belonged to the 31-year-old from Mantes-la-Jolie, whose home region is not far from where this race will finish in 12 days' time, and this afternoon in the Savoie department of the Rhône-Alpes region he took a win that will remain with him long after the conclusion of the 97th Tour de France in Paris on July 25.

Having spent much of the day in a high-powered break, Casar climbed the Col de la Colombière, Col de Aravis, Col des Saisies and the Col de la Madeleine ahead of the peloton - by day's end he had outsprinted fellow escapees Luis León Sanchez (Caisse d'Epargne) and Damiano Cunego (Lampre-Farnese Vini) to add another victory to the one he earned on stage 18 of the 2007 Tour de France in Angoulême.

Le JO'G Stage 9 2010		Le Tour Stage 9 2010
Cummertrees - Stair		Morzine-Avoriaz -
		Saint Jean-de Maurienne
		Winner Casar
Distance	71.795 miles	127.813 miles
Time Cycling	5hr.31m.04s.	5hr.8m.10s.
Average Speed	13.0 mph.	24.89 mph.

Stage 10

Friday 6th August Stair to Clachan

Up early for breakfast, good it was too, with wonderfully cooked poached eggs on well buttered toast, it was only then we found out, from mine host that the burglar alarm had been set off in the small hours of the morning, didn't we know. When he said he had been called out by the police to check the premises and assured us nothing was amiss, presumably meaning the bike was safe.

It was only then I thought about the lack of cars in the car park as I peered out earlier and as we looked around the dining room, our table was the only one laid out for breakfast, which only served as confirmation that we had been alone and locked in the pub over night with a fully stocked bar but of course with a burglar alarm to contend with!

As I set off, after the revelation of spending a night in the Stair Inn alone, the day was cloudy with a prospect of rain later, today I did not need sun cream.. However, I had good vibes for this stage as the wind, although not strong was still at my back and I bowled along at a decent pace once again enjoying some lovely lowland Scottish scenery.

Soon I was in the small town of Tarbolton whose claim to fame for me, was that the Scottish rugby union prop forward of the seventies John "Ian" McLaughlan aka Mighty Mouse was born and bred there. He provided me with some great entertainment over the years watching him on television with the great Bill Maclaren of the BBC commentating as he took part in the Five Nations Rugby Tournament as it was then called. Back to the cycling and the A730 was taking me through some lovely countryside when after crossing the A77 I soon rode into the town of Dundonald which reminded me of an earlier town I had visited in Eire, Ballymote. It had the same wide road with plenty of parking diagonally at the kerb, with no dreaded yellow lines the curse of the modern day motorist.

After passing through the town it all went a bit awry, at the ironically named village of Drybridge a mile further on, it rained and rained and rained. A quote from Brian London, a famous English boxer came to mind; after fighting Muhammad Ali or Cassius Clay as he was then , who was extremely quick for a big man, he said,
"I knew he was quick but not that b----y quick!"
Today I could say,
"I knew I would get wet in Scotland but not that b----y wet!"

Apart from the bad weather the lovely scenery also took a distinctive nose dive after crossing the River Irvine, I ended up on the A78, a major trunk road cutting through the industrial heartlands of Irvine, Kilwinning, Saltcoats and the port of Ardrossan. It was a long 9 miles on this road, the A30 to Exeter came to mind. It was a similar situation, very narrow cycle path full of detritus from the carriageway with lorries and cars thundering by at 70mph plus, it was akin to riding on a yard wide hard shoulder on the M6, not my finest hour. However, compared to George and Arthur - two intrepid members of the 2002 Kenyan Commonwealth Games cycling team it was a walk in the park.

They were based at the Manchester athletes' village, but were due to compete in a road race at Rivington, near Bolton. The Kenyan team arrived in England without their bikes, because they were in such bad shape, but was helped out by a generous cycle shop owner who lent them some wheels.

Ever enthusiastic, George and Arthur grabbed a map which revealed a nice blue road leading almost directly to their destination, so they braved the incessant honking of long-haul truckers, the erratic driving of stressed caravanners and even the danger of our speeding royals to check out the venue. Amazingly, they reached their destination safely, and luxuriated in their Lancastrian surroundings before heading back to base and the nice blue road on the map, you've guessed it, the M61!

At times I felt a bit like George and Arthur but it was only a means to an end, probably the least enjoyable part of my journey, thankfully it only lasted the few miles but it seemed like forever. Finally I came to the last roundabout and for a mile it was a downward stretch to the glorious sea. The Firth of Clyde north west of Ardrossan saved my life, what a sight to drop down a hill from the big road onto the sea in front of you not five yards away, magical to me. I've always loved the briny waters and it gave me a great lift after a miserable hour on a miserable road.

I remembered a Caribbean holiday spent in Barbados with my family a few years ago now. We hired a car for a few days and I found myself driving along a road only five or six yards away from the sea with a lovely narrow beach of white sand in between. It might have been a bit bluer, a bit calmer and the weather a bit sunnier than what I was looking at but at that moment I would take anything to cheer me up.

The road now turned northwards a great direction for me with the wind at my back and the rain finally easing up. I made good time through West Kilbride and another eight miles or so to Largs my next stop for lunch. I began to feel better and better, amazing what little things can do to lighten up your life, a sight of the sea, no rain the wind at my back but as yet no sun.

I reached Largs in good time but got a message from my outside caterer that lunch would be served on the promenade as it was the only place to park. I enjoyed my grub once again in glorious Victorian surroundings within sight of the sea and believe it or not the sun made a fleeting appearance.

After lunch I replaced my wet cycling jacket and gloves and I felt like a new man on my way to the ferry at Gourock, or to be more accurate McInroy's Point to cross the Firth of Clyde to Hunter's Quay. As I left, Mary went into town to get money and provisions from a Morrisons supermarket leaving me to head north once again, 15 miles to Gourock the sign said.

The road surface was superb and it followed the sea with only yards in between. I was making great time when another cyclist on an immaculate road bike wearing a gleaming pro-team jersey passed me just outside of Largs without as much as a by your leave, did I shirk the challenge? of course not, it was *Mano a Mano* my English Cavendish to his Scottish Millar! I was feeling good and enjoyed tracking him, did he look back? No but if he had he would have seen the biggest smirk across anyone's face he had ever seen. As I was about to do my Cav special for the line I was thwarted by some road works' traffic lights on red, at this he U-turned back to Largs with a sly glance across, moral victory to me I think.

On green I made my way more leisurely to Selmorlie a little village on the coast a few miles further on. Apparently it was here in the early part of the 1900s out on the Firth that the Royal Navy set a nautical mile to check the speed of their new warships, it was called the 'Selmorlie mile'. The speed I had just been travelling three minutes would have been enough for me.

From here to Weymiss point which sticks out considerably, I lost sight of the sea but came across what I thought was a Baker's Convention, all I could see from my position on the bike were lots of white trilby style hats just showing above a hedge, further on through a gate all was revealed, a game of bowls of the flat green variety. Back to the coast at Inverkip quite a pleasant little village then inland I turned left down the A770 to McInroy's Point for the ferry terminal at breakneck speed to arrive with a great average of well over 15 mph.

Having arrived at the ferry port my concern was that Mary had not passed me on the only road from Larg, was the car playing up I wondered or was I in the wrong place? I decided to ask the ferry man at the gate as to whether I was actually at the correct terminal for Hunter's Quay ferry. He affirmed I was so Mary was missing in action. A phone call was not returned but before I could get really worried the black Mondeo breezed into the car park minutes later. When I asked her about her late arrival, thankfully nothing was amiss apparently I had just blown her away with my speed! Did I feel just like Mark Cavendish or what? I had time to savour the moment for the ferry had not yet arrived, little did I know that this great feeling was to be obliterated with the weather later on.

Having boarded the ferry I got chatting with a local from Dunoon although he now lived in America and was over for a visit. After explaining what I was doing he told a tale of a man who was from my neck of the woods, Skelmersdale a new town built close by to where I live. His name was Dr. Geebers who had been written about in the local press as a homeless man walking around the British Isles creating sculptures from local materials on the beaches in local parks or wherever he can.

Having seen some of his efforts on the internet since, he was definitely not in the league of Charles Jencks the American landscape architect who produced the Goddess of the North in Northumberland in 2010, however I could not fault his efforts. He lived on hand outs and was writing a book about his exploits the profits of which were to go to a homeless charity. It was an interesting conversation one which would come back to haunt me later.

He also told me of a beautiful loch that I would pass, Eck which according to him was the most scenic in Scotland, was he a wee bit biased do you think? This man was a mine of information on the locale; the next bit was about a couple of pubs by the side of the loch, the Coylett Inn and the Whistlefield Inn. The Coylett was frequented by the actress Emma Thompson who apparently lives close by some of the year and she used the place as her local. The Whistlefield further up the loch was a pub that held folk music sessions and he would be joining them that night.

Finally we docked, the ferry journey and the rest period were over and we disembarked at the port of Hunter's Quay with the black clouds looming large over the forthcoming hills. Having got myself together I set off again on terra firma around the harbour on the shores of Holy Loch a place made famous in the sixties by the CND organisation.

During World War II, this loch was used as a submarine base and from 1961–1992 it was used as a US Polaris nuclear submarine base when the Ban the Bomb people got involved. In 1992, the Holy Loch base was deemed unnecessary following the demise of the Soviet Union and subsequently withdrawn; to be honest it didn't look big enough for all those subs anyway.

There was a slight drizzle as I rode around Holy loch which turned to rain as I reached the small village of Dalinlongart at the head of the loch. I took shelter beneath a tree and demolished a biscuit but the rain did not abate, if anything it got worse, so off I set again with clenched teeth and grim determination against the elements.

My spirits lifted when I saw a road sign informing me of only 13 miles to go to Clachan my overnight stop. 13 miles was nothing on my own turf but it turned out to feel more like 33 miles in the rain which by now was pouring incessantly.

I continued in my determined fashion along the road to Clachan and soon I reached Loch Eck, I won't be childish enough to use the pun 'by eck it was beautiful' but it certainly was all that I had been led to believe and no doubt even better on a sunnier day. However today the mist rolled over the hills surrounding the loch like a window blind being pulled down shutting out the view and it still rained. There was no sign of dear Emma as I neared the Coylett Inn, perhaps the rain was too much or could she already be inside knocking back the grog! I felt too wet to check and if I stopped to go inside the pub would I ever get out again? I trundled on.

The rain persisted, I was wet through and soon lost interest in the 'beautiful' surroundings I now slogged my way along the loch side finally reaching the turn off to the Whistlefield Inn after 3 miles making it now only six to go. I left the loch soon after and found myself bisecting the Glenbranter Forest, this must be heaven for the dreaded midge but not today unless they have swim shorts or a bikini!

At long last the road sign for Clachan came into view with a poster advert for the local pub that sounded good. Soon I came to the top of a long hill going down, I stopped to check the map of the whereabouts of the mystical Old Manse, couldn't tell where it was. I looked down the long hill and decided I needed help, there was no way I was going down the hill to find that the B&B was back at the top.

After consulting a garage attendant down the hill I went to find Mary round the corner (you can say round the bend if you want to) waiting with camera in hand. I dismounted to be told the sinister tale of the mother's house at the Bates Motel in Psycho being transferred to Clachan for the summer! Mary prepared me for an eccentric stay.

When putting together the B & Bs for the trip I had the Devil's own job in finding one in this area, very few and far between. I did manage to find this, the Old

Manse, on Tripadvisor it was given the Carlsberg treatment by one of the contributors, probably the best B&B in Scotland. However I could not find the telephone number, e-mail or even an address, shades of Hotel California to me! I persevered and finally I had them all. I e-mailed, no answer. I rang, no answer. I rang many times, no answer. I wrote a letter, you've guessed it, no answer. I had by now given up and was looking for other accommodation which was not easy, it meant another 20 or so miles in the day, then an e-mail arrived;

Dear Graham,

Thank you for your letter and Email. My husband and I have just spent four days on the Shetland Islands – hence the delay in replying to you.............etc.etc.

With best wishes
  Sheila

Thank heavens for normality, that was the history of the house and now for the reality of Bates Motel, you could imagine how Mary felt. When she arrived in the car at the door to the house there was no-one around but by the time she got to the boot of the car for her luggage the owners were standing there to greet her,
"You must be Mrs. Forrester....... tea?"
      A little perturbed what with the problems of finding the place and in communication, Mary declined the offer and decided that there would be safety in numbers so explained she would go looking for me on the road after registering. So it was with some apprehension I made my way up the hill to the 'Bates Motel' but we couldn't have been more wrong.

On arrival at the house I was met by Mr. and Mrs. Macpherson with a similar greeting that Mary had, "Come in get out of those wet clothes and have some tea and biscuits."

I decided it was a great offer, anything to get out of these wet clothes which were getting decidedly chilly having stopped my exertions. A quick change and down to the parlour where a wood fire was burning in the hearth, mine host, Rob, telling me that I was in charge and in no way was I to let it out! no pressure then. Sheila brought in a tray full of cakes and biscuits with a large pot of tea with china cups what a splendid way to wind down the rainy afternoon and what a generous and kindly couple.

After tea we had a wash and brush up and made our way to the local pub as advertised near the road sign. It turned out to be the Clachan Arms and reminded me of the local shop for local people in the series 'League of Gentlemen'. No food served here was the reply to my question of a menu but I was informed of the Whistlefield Inn about 5 miles away up from the shores of Loch Eck, I knew it well and it was 6 miles, off we went, we seemed to be drawn to the pub, would we run into the chap from the ferry?

It certainly was a lively place the folk singers in full swing. The food was excellent, no sign of the 'local' and after a few drinks we made our way back to Bates' and our bed. It was a wonderfully appointed bedroom in the Victorian style with numerous books to read and his and hers bathrobes which seemed a one size fits all except of course our size, one would have done for the pair of us. We both had a good laugh but more to the point a good night's sleep in the peaceful surroundings and no dreams of motel 'drag queens'!

Two French riders in a day-long break, Bastille Day and the Tour de France... it would have been an irresistible mix, except that Sergio Paulinho hadn't read the script. Team RadioShack's Portuguese domestique salvaged something from this year's Tour with victory in Gap this afternoon, dashing the dreams of the locals.

Fairy tales are called so for a reason - they don't happen often - and while a French winner today would have capped what has been thus far a fantastic Tour for local riders, with the exploits of Sylvain Chavanel and yesterday's stage victory for Sandy Casar, Cinderella's pumpkin was used to make soup rather than carry a local rider to a triumph in the shadow of the Alps.

Paulinho's daring in the final 10km of the stage deserved the victory it garnered however, the 30-year-old fighting for line honours with Caisse d'Epargne's Vasili Kiryienka and pipping the Belarusian at the post in what was a tight finish.
"I knew I had to attack to get away from the group, and I actually felt pretty good," Paulinho said after the stage.
"I was just a little bit stronger than Kiryienka, and waited until the last moment to make my move."

Le JO'G Stage 10 2010		Le Tour Stage 10 2010
Stair - Clachan		Chambery - Gap
		Winner Paulinho
Distance	65.082 miles	111.875 miles
Time Cycling	4hr.21m.02s.	5hr.10m.56s.
Average Speed	15.0 mph.	21.59 mph.

Stage 11

We both awoke still alive then, nothing from 'Norman Bates' during the night. After a quick wash we went down for breakfast which had been ordered through Rob the previous day while we enjoyed his hospitality with tea, cakes and his wood fire.

He asked us what we wanted and continued to rhyme off an enormous list of food, literally anything we asked for he would supply. I was a bit bemused by it all and ordered my usual porridge then poached eggs on toast with toast and marmalade to follow. He maintained it would be the best porridge I had ever tasted cooked that morning by the fair hand of Sheila and the poached eggs would be sublime cooked by him. Mary throughout all this chat with a bit more time and more agile of mind, plumped for smoked salmon and all the trimmings.

The breakfast of course, was magnificent. It was spent in the delightful company of an American couple from Gettysburg as we sat around a large table laid out with silverware looking like something from Downton Abbey. They informed us that they were on a walking holiday with a group of other people of different nationalities, I was just glad they didn't say they were *doing* Argyll. We had a good chat and when the conversation turned to what I was doing he made it plain I should not try to cycle in America, far too dangerous as the trucks just didn't care about cyclists.

Unfortunately James Cracknell, the Olympic rowing gold medallist of 2000 and 2004, can attest to that having been knocked off his bike outside of the town of Winslow in Arizona when a petrol tanker's wing mirror clipped the back of his cycle helmet the following month in September, he should have spoken to my American friend first. He was in the process of shooting a television series where he had to cycle, run and row across the US in 16 or 18 days depending what you read, a bit quicker than me then.

After the wonderful breakfast I had to tear myself away unfortunately, to continue *my little* journey northwards to Port Appin my next stop. Since there was no kettle in our room to boil the water for the lunchtime coffee I went to ask Rob for some boiling water. When he found out what it was for he said he would make up the flask,
"Instant coffee would do," I suggested,
"We don't do instant," he replied. Of course not, silly me.

Having spent time chatting to our friends from across the pond it became a latish start, also time was spent waiting for the rest of the cosmopolitan walking group, who had assembled outside, to say their goodbyes. It was 9.40am, before I got going, down the hill and onto the road heading for the open wilderness that is the Highlands of Scotland.

The first part of the journey was not wild at all, on the coastal road around the wonderful Loch Fyne. How beautiful it was to travel by the side of these waters so tranquil, my first stop was to be the town of

Inverary about 20 miles away but only 2 as the crow flies or the boat sails, oh for a bridge. After 5 or 6 miles I moved inland at St. Catherines to trundle up a longish slope but I felt so good I almost didn't know I was going uphill! I changed roads onto the A83 after crossing Kinglas Water moving around to the head of the loch. From here I double backheading for Inverary 8 miles away. There are magnificent views all over the place and reflections that are magical just magical.

I finally arrived in the town to meet my first problem of the day, according to my map I needed to turn right onto the A819 but the only road I saw seemed to go through a supermarket car park, can't be right, I thought it must be further on. So further on I go and pass two gentlemen, obviously local, sitting enjoying watching the world and me go by.

Another few hundred yards and I realised I was going in the wrong direction. Round the church which appeared in the centre of the road and had lost its spire in the 1930s, I made my way back to the same turning, I don't know what the two old gents must have been thinking. However, I was approaching the turn from the opposite side now and I could see that it passed the car park and moved onto a hill 1 in 7 up, of course.

My despair was short lived as I heard the sound of bagpipes, for the first time in Scotland, travelling on the wind from behind a local Kirk, it appeared they were practising for a wedding later that day. The road did go up but gratifyingly not for long so I was soon off again at a goodish lick on my way to lunch in Lochawe. Soon the road started its 4 mile ascent over the hill aptly named the 'Craig nan sassanach', which I translated to be 'Crag of the English', could be wrong I suppose. My legs began to tire with the hill and the heat as I desperately looked for landmarks around me to check my position on the map and the distance from the top. I just kept going and eventually I made the summit for a well earned stop and a drink, once again I found myself in the middle of nowhere, so quiet with no cars to spoil the silence.

It was now payback time, down the hill I went like the best in Le Tour, this was much better, downhill with the sun on my back what more could I want. I whizzed down the hill to reach Loch Awe and then the junction with the A85, a quick turn left and I was soon into the village of Lochawe for my most excellent lunch courtesy of my lady wife. The sun was now shining almost constantly and the views from this morning's ride were simply breathtaking. The ride around Loch Fyne and then Loch Awe to lunch was just superb, with more to come around the sea Loch Etive to Connel I couldn't wait.

Lunch was soon finished and I was on my way again around the loch side and then through the pass of Brander with massive mountains, fells call them what you will but I was glad I was travelling along the river Awe certainly in awe of my surroundings, the high mountains are coming.

Along the pass I came across the Cruachan Power Station, which is buried almost 1km below the ground in a massive cavern, as high as the Tower of London. It houses enormous turbines converting water into electricity so the blurb on the board outside explained, I certainly needed my own energy so I took the opportunity whilst stopped, for a bar, fruit and grain that is and a drink.

In about 3 miles I crossed the river at the Bridge of Awe a small hamlet and made my way to the larger village of Tanuilt by the river Nant. The wind today was not strong, gusting about 12 mph but it was coming from the WNW which was my direction of travel from Tanuilt on my way to the town of Connel. It had started to become a real irritation and so when I reached a downhill stretch on the road just before the railway bridge at Stonefield I decided to let go.

I did not let go for long though, the road surface was so bad it was akin to riding on a miniature Giant's Causeway, I had to slow right down to about 7 or 8 mph to save my body but especially my bike from being shaken to pieces it was just disgraceful. This lasted for far too long, I was afraid my bike would sustain some permanent damage and I was considering getting off and pushing when suddenly the road surface became like glass but now slightly uphill, I was so angry with the local council I sped away as fast as I could to disperse my wrath but ended up merely tiring myself out, what a waste of energy another muesli bar please.

By now I was on the coast of the sea loch Etive which had a calming influence and I felt much more comfortable with myself. On turning round a small promontory what a view assailed my eyes, the Connel Bridge, There it was in front of me, with the sun glinting off the loch the steel battleship grey bridge making a statement across the Falls of Lora, a marvellous sight the terrible road surface a distant memory. Unfortunately the falls were not happening today as the tide was in with the sea and the loch at the same level but a splendid view nevertheless. Another couple of miles and I was on the bridge's approach road riding northwards across its span. This afforded great views back along the loch and also out to sea to the islands of Eilean Mòr and Lismore beyond.

Having crossed the bridge I stopped to take my bearings, a drink and a snack and just digest the wonderful scenery roundabouts as well as the wheat bar. Looking at my map it told me I was now travelling north which meant the pesky wind was less of a hindrance and the sun more of a blessing. I am now on the A828 skirting Ardmucknish Bay to my left on my way to the next town of Benderloch. From here I was soon into the town of Barcaldine which I would visit again before the day was out.

It's a hop skip and a jump and a few hills now to Appin, across the bridge over Loch Creran I took the high road to the village (high is a euphemism for hilly in these parts). I reached Appin wondering where Mary was for I couldn't easily tell from my map where the B&B was located. I turned left for the Port area, which was off my route and moseyed on down the lane at a leisurely pace and the views were absolutely tremendous I'm running out of hyperboles to describe these areas.

The Castle Stalker in the bay against the setting sun was just breathtaking. Eventually I reached a small lane to my right which said Fasghad B&B must be the one and turned. I could go on and on about the scenery and the sea views from this place but it would just be a bore so I'll shut up and think only of my memories.

Mary was there of course with the ubiquitous camera for the shot of finishing the stage. She then informed me that the owners of the bungalow were not there, my head dropped but hold on there was a note attached to the front door of the house for the two sets of residentees, us being one. The note said to use the key in the door to the B&B part of the house and then the Forresters to go to room 4 we will be back shortly! Could leaving a house unlocked for most of the day happen anywhere else? I think not, truly amazing.

Later on in the day the owners son came around suffering from a tremendous hangover, when asked he informed us of two places to eat, one of which he didn't recommend in the port area unless you were celebrating an anniversary or something unbelievably pricey he informed us. So we settled for his best choice a large pub close to the bridge over the loch I passed on the way in.

A good rest then a clean up and we were ready to take on some food. Off we go to the recommended eating house only to be told we should have booked as they were full but we could have sat outside with the millions of other guests flying on the wing waiting for their blood tit bit, thanks mate for not telling us, his hangover must have mushed his brain. Remember Barcaldine I said I would visit again here it comes.

Down the road the way I came to find somewhere to eat, unbelievably there was nowhere to be found except on entering the town we saw a sign pointing to a Fish and Chip shop on a Caravan Park, by now I was hungry and that had to do. It was a van really and of course there was a queue. Whilst waiting for my order I was bitten to death by our friendly local midges, I really cannot understand how the locals cope with these, however the chips were good and filled my belly, time to head back to Fasghad.

When we arrived back at the guest house the absent owners had turned up and told us they had been out for the day with their elder son and family on the beach. They were sorry for their lateness in coming back but they had decided to call for a Chinese Takeaway to eat at their son's house before returning! Time for bed I thought but to reflect on the stage; it was definitely a day for sun cream, completely the opposite of yesterday.

It was a day that showed Scotland at its best with the magnificent grandeur of high fells and superb loch views, absolutely wonderful, more please.

For most people, 13 is an unlucky number. Fabian Cancellara famously wears the dossard bearing that numeral upside down to avoid its potential misfortune. This afternoon in Bourg-lès-Valence however, it was a lucky number for Mark Cavendish as he took his 13th win and went into the history books - he has now won the most Tour de France stages of any current sprinter. The stage was overshadowed when Cavendish's teammate, Mark Renshaw, was thrown out of the race for head-butting Julian Dean (Garmin-Transitions)

However, by winning Cavendish has beaten the record held by his mentor, Erik Zabel, who previously held the record whilst a professional, with 12 stage wins in la grande boucle. Cavendish did it in the style to which we've become accustomed, the HTC-Columbia sprinter continuing to gain confidence in this year's race after a shaky start.

He had to go from a long way out to earn the victory though, courtesy of a coming together between Antipodean duo Mark Renshaw and Julian Dean in the final 500 metres. In a sign of his increasing sprinting maturity, Cavendish saw the opportunity to dash for double the distance he normally would - almost 400 metres - and backed himself to get the job done.

"Julian came and he was fighting with Mark at the finish and

It left me boxed in if he'd have pushed him across, as soon as I saw a gap I had to go," said Cavendish after the finish.

"Normally I go with 200 or 250 [metres] maximum and at 375 metres to go I saw a gap... it wasn't so much a sprint but a little breakaway, well, by my standards anyway! It was hard, actually... It was a really, really long way to the finish.

Le JO'G Stage 11 2010	Le Tour Stage 11 2010
Clachan – Port Appin	Sisteron – Bourg-les-Valence
	Winner Cavendish

Distance	67.316 miles	115.313 miles
Time Cycling	4hr.51m.07s.	4hr.42m.29s.
Average Speed	13.9 mph.	24.49 mph

Stage 12

Sunday 8th August Port Appin to Fort Augustus

The first time I heard sheep bleating so early in the morning was in Wales when camping with my friend Colin before we did a long distance walk taking in Tryfan. They surrounded the tent at about five in the morning, I was not best pleased.

This morning I awoke again to sheep bleating for the second time but now they were outside my bedroom window a lovely sound much better than an alarm clock, I felt refreshed and it certainly beat the dawn chorus. As I opened the curtains and looked out I saw the early morning sun glint off Loch Linnhe not half a mile away, I promised no more hyperboles didn't I? I'll shut up now.

We arrived at breakfast to share the dining room with the other family who had arrived yesterday, they originally hailed from Liverpool although from their accents you couldn't tell. They had been to one of the Islands off the west coast and were now making their way back home somewhere down south. Fed and feeling full of energy I got myself ready and went to retrieve my bike.

Oh dear, I noticed the rear tyre was a little flat let down, a little like I felt. Mmmmm, was it the 'so called mended' puncture causing more problems? I wondered whether to change the inner tube but the midges were absolutely dreadful, they were having a feast on my face, I needed to get away and fast. I pumped up the tyre as quickly as I could, virtually with my eyes closed against the attack from the bloodsuckers. Fortunately it seemed to hold and I rushed back inside away from the eating frenzy. I was finally off at the late time of 9.20 although that mattered little for it was only a shortish journey today.

There was an early morning chill to the air but the two miles back to the main route warmed me up somewhat. The landlady had told me of a large hill on the road in the direction I was travelling, really looking forward to that! Still I was on my way to the Highlands, the big mountains of Nevis and company, Fort William here I come this was what it was all about.

The hill turned out to be 1 in 8 but of no real length and no real trouble to the hardened rider I was becoming, don't get me wrong I didn't exactly go up like Schleck or Contador on the Col du Toumalet but nice and easy worked. It was then down to another loch side road with very light traffic to spoil my efforts perhaps early Sunday morning had something to do with that.

I felt really good in the early sunshine cycling along the coast road, 28 miles to the lunch stop beneath the Ben in Fort William easy, nobbut a cock stride. Soon the road turned inland to avoid Ardsheal Hill and then onto the village of Kentallen where I stopped to find a likely spot to empty my bladder.

At this point in the journey I would like to tell you how I abhor cycle routes. The people who design them seem to be having a laugh at the cyclist's expense. They go all around the houses at roundabouts and on and off pavements and are usually full of life's detritus. Personally I would rather take my chances with the traffic although I appreciate James Cracknell and his family may not agree. I tell you this because when I stopped to look for a toilet or bush I was eyeing up a tarmac track on a lower level than me when a car suddenly pulled up in the middle of the road. The window came down and the driver in a strong Scottish accent pointed to the track and said,

"Yes that is a cycle path and I wish the b----y cyclists around here would b----y use the damn thing. It goes all the way to Ballachulish Bridge and it's b----y quiet with no b----y traffic."

How could I refuse such a wonderful invitation? Even with my own misgivings about cycle tracks I now looked at it in a different light, so with cars piling up behind him the drivers just slightly losing their temper, I thought this was as good a time as any to be off. I thanked him and went down to use the track for more things than riding a bike.

The man, however was spot on, it was a wonderful track with a decent road surface for cycling. I happily tootled along until the path crossed under the road via a tunnel and wound its way up into woodland. Now I have never liked woods for finding your way when I used to go walking, as the saying goes, you cannot see the wood for the trees and that is all you see, no landmarks to help guide you through. This is exactly what happened here, what did I say about cycle tracks?

Up and down I went round and round I went and of course there were no signs what would be the point of that? I became, I must confess a little cross, as my old deputy head used to say. I wandered around and came to a crossroads, which way to go, again no signs, I heard voices and rode quickly towards them. It was a golf course and fortunately there were two golfers in close proximity to the path. I asked the way and thankfully they knew, I set off and finally made it to the main road, the A82.

Once again having left the cycle track there was no sign to denote the way and by now I was totally disorientated. I set off one way to a road sign which faced the opposite way, after riding beneath it to the other side I now knew I should be going in the opposite direction. If anybody asks why cyclists do not use cycle paths this is a prime example.

There would be only one thing to get me out of my anger and that would be a wonderful bridge at Ballachulish, there was, perhaps not quite wonderful but certainly noteworthy. Like the Connel Bridge it was made of steel perhaps not quite as grand but it sat well between the lochs Linnhe and Leven and had a great view on the crossing. On the other side of the bridge I passed through North Ballachulish travelling eastwards with the wind at my back. I turned north east just after Onich and started riding the coast road all the way to the Highland town of Fort William.

The best-laid schemes o' mice an' men gang aft agley, wrote the great Rabbie Burns in his poem about finding a nest of mice after ploughing up the field, so legend as it. Well my *scheme* for lunch certainly went *agley* in Fort William. The plan was to meet Mary in a whisky distillery's visitor centre (I thought this to be a good idea) just through the town, as the Muskrats say, simples. I followed my map through the town and then out of the town no Mary, no distillery, I stopped on a garage forecourt and got on the phone,
"Where are you?" I asked.

131

She told me that she had already been to the distillery and that they would be closing the gates soon so she had made her way back into the town and was now stationed at a car park in the centre.

She gave me instructions on how to get there. I closed the phone but everything she said didn't seem to make sense it just seemed in the wrong direction. After more phone calls and then after asking the garage attendant as to the whereabouts of the distillery, which was just across the road! What an idiot, I suddenly twigged that she had arrived at the distillery another way because of the sat nav route and then it all became clear to my muddled mind, as I said what an idiot.

I turned around and made my way back into the town to be hailed down by Mary from the car park, at last lunch. We sat eating another extra special meal in gorgeous sunshine sat on a bench in a park close by. The 'talents' of would be Lee Westwoods and Luke Donalds on a putting green kept us amused throughout. Looking up from the bench I could see we were in the shadow of the Ben bringing back memories of years back when I was a lad of 15 attempting to scale the mountain, well at least walk up it.

Fort William was a different place then, almost fifty years ago it has certainly blossomed since. I camped for a week with a Boy's Club from Liverpool just outside of the town by the river Nevis. The journey up from home took almost 24 hours in the back of a beat up minibus which had to tackle the hills on the roads in reverse with us walking! We attempted the walk up the Ben after breakfast one morning but got only two thirds of the way up before everyone either got the runs or vomited, I blame the sausages, oh happy days.

Well here I was again on a different challenge talking of which I needed to be off. Again it was on the A82 taking me on the edge of Leanachan Forest for six miles to Spean Bridge. This village is probably best known for its memorial to the Commandos atop a long hill and a fine one it is too. They and the United States Army Rangers were trained in the area around the village between 1942 and 1945. When my wife was there she saw Japanese tourists having their photographs taken below the memorial in front of an inscription, United We Conquer, how ironic.

From here I continued on the 'A' road vying with a Frenchman, not for long, he was unfortunately a much better cyclist than I and he left me for dead. Back I went down to the loch side but this time it was Loch Lochy, imaginative name that. Along this road I cycled with great views of forests on both sides of the loch and soon I was at the Laggan Locks on the Caledonian Canal, here the road crosses to the other side and in three miles I was in the small village of Invergarry on the banks of Loch Oich.

At the end of this loch I crossed the Caledonian Canal again and continued on General Wades Military Road (A82) absolutely steaming now on a slightly downhill stretch on this good straight road. I am the winner of the stage if I could speed up; of course I could and creamed it into the town. I rang Mary to tell her I was half a mile away then shot off and round the corner I caught her running to the viewpoint at Morag's Lodge our hostel for the night. She got the picture.

The hostel was well appointed with free internet access allowing me to get the weather conditions from Metcheck for the next few days. After a shower and wind down we hit the town for food and drink. The place was packed with tourists all pubs and cafes full of people wanting to eat. Rather than wait we decided to eat al fresco on the charming and picturesque locks of the Caledonian Canal where it pours into Loch Ness. Fish and chips never tasted so good. The food was washed down with a couple of pints of best bitter whilst watching the foreign tourists struggle with pounds sterling, what would they have been like with pounds shillings and pence?

Joaquin Rodriguez (Team Katusha) out-sprinted Alberto Contador (Astana) to take a thrilling victory in Mende at the end of stage 12 of the Tour de France. The Spanish duo escaped on the steep slopes of the Montée Laurent Jalabert in the finale to an enthralling day's racing that saw minor but potentially telling chinks exposed in the armour of yellow jersey Andy Schleck and his Saxo Bank team. The Luxembourg rider lost ten seconds to Contador, who laid down an important psychological marker ahead of the duo's expected showdown in the Pyrenees.

At the foot of the final climb the peloton trailed the four survivors of the day's early breakaway by 40 seconds, and the gap remained stable as Alexandre Vinokourov (Astana) dropped first Ryder Hesjedal (Garmin-Transitions) and then Andreas Kloden (RadioShack), before finally edging clear of Vasily Kyrienka (Caisse d'Epargne). Accelerations from Jean Gadret (Ag2r) and Jurgen Van den Broeck (Omega Pharma – Lotto) made no dent in his lead, and it seemed inevitable that the Kazakh was about to win a stage in his first Tour appearance since returning a positive test for blood doping in 2007. Two kilometres from the line, however, Rodriguez lit the blue touch paper behind with a tentative attack, and Contador responded with an explosive acceleration of his own.

He immediately opened a gap of five bike lengths on Andy Schleck, who appeared caught off guard by the ferocity of the Spaniard's move. Worse was to follow for the Luxembourger. Having attempted to counter the break, Schleck found that he didn't have the legs to sustain such a pace. While Rodriguez managed to hold Contador's wheel, Schleck was forced to let Van den Broeck take up the chase.

Up front, there was an air of inevitability about the finish. If Rodriguez was unable to contribute to pace-setting duties with Contador on the climb itself, in the final kilometre he was simply unwilling to do so, and he timed his sprint to perfection to come around the double Tour winner on the line.

Le JO'G Stage 12 2010		Le Tour Stage 12 2010
Port Appin – Fort Augustus		Bourg-de Piage - Mende
		Winner Rodriguez
Distance	62.349 miles	131.56 miles
Time Cycling	4hr.08m.02s.	4hr.58m.26s.
Average Speed	15.2 mph.	26.45 mph

Stage 13

Monday 9th August Fort Augustus to Bonar Bridge

Before I begin to describe this stage, which just happened to be stage 13, although not superstitious, unlike Cancellara, I have to say that in all the thousands of miles I have cycled this probably was my worst ever day on a bike for a variety of reasons, least of all that I did not see the Loch Ness Monster but please read on for my litany of problems on this Black Monday.

It all started when I organised the route from the CTC at least six months before the actual trip. The route took me along the A82 by the side of Loch Ness but instead of going the full length to Inverness it cut off at the village of Drumnadrochit to go over the tops to Beauly. I wondered at the time as to the reasons but probably traffic would have been bad going into Inverness or the town itself would have been too busy or possibly the person who devised this route had a vicious sense of humour.

The A833 from the village seemed to go up very quickly and the only thing I could see on the map were two chevrons in the space of about one kilometer, which could only mean one thing to me, a steep hill! I was not looking forward to this from six months before the ride and now it was nearly upon me I was becoming increasingly anxious that I wouldn't make it without having to stop. I couldn't see Andy Schleck getting off and pushing his bike up the Col du Soulor in the

Pyrenees and so in my eyes if I did that here I would have failed the challenge, what mental pressure I put myself under even before I started the stage, where are the Sports Psychologists when you need one?

That was my first problem before I even got on the bike.

The stage started well in Morag's Lodge, the breakfast was good with plenty of porridge, cereal and toast with copious cups of coffee to keep my caffeine levels up. After packing up and paying up we emerged from the hostel into a dull miserable overcast sort of day threatening rain which held off until I sat on my bike. The forecast was for showers in the morning with rain in the afternoon I hoped this was just one of those showers.

Astride my bike I wondered whether to go to the toilet one more time remember the bowels of a cyclist are in a delicate balance, well mine are anyway without giving too much information away. Could I be bothered to undress fully because of my bib shorts, nah I'd be okay or so I thought. I set off with drizzle in the air hoping it would not get much worse but before I got to the main road I realised I'd forgotten my snacks for the journey whoops! Not a good start.

Settling into a reasonable rhythm once again on the A82, although the drizzle and the roller coaster road didn't help, I still felt the pull of the toilet, should have gone again before setting off, bad decision. This was very unusual for me, did I have a duff pint the previous night? What to do what to do? Well I knew what to do, I needed a spot away from prying eyes but yet in some sort of clearing in the Portclair Forest I was travelling through. Clearings were definitely at a premium and time had got the better of me but we were in the land of the midge and this was a lovely habitat for the little beggars. I knew when I stopped that it would have to be quick, in and out like a commando raid before they have the chance to bite, Ha, that didn't work.

Now remember everything had to come off, because of the bib shorts unfortunately. I considered the problems of being naked in a swarm of these biting insects and decided to go for it and do everything as quickly as possible. No sooner had I got in there than they rose up from the ground and swarmed around me, the wee beasties could not believe their luck, the soft white flesh of an Englishman fee fi fo fum! I was out of there tout suite but I was still savaged by the bloodsuckers especially on my left fleshy buttock, probably trapped a few of the beggars when I pulled up my trolleys in haste, oh the pain!

The relief in my bowels however, was palpable (too much information?) anyway I set off again and was doing rather well time wise and swiftly moved down to the shores of the Loch, at least I had the view to take my mind off the itching that was starting up under my shorts. I glanced across at the water and the mist began to rise showing a long ripple could it be………? Of course not, don't be silly.

The rain that was supposed to be showery became more constant and my speed took a bit of a tumble with the downpour and the up and down of the road getting no less, fortunately the traffic was particularly light so making it easier to ride on the narrowish road in places and thankfully no caravans. After another four or five miles or so I turned away from the loch to the village of Invermoriston which sported an enormous car and coach park with, you've guessed it, toilet facilities where you could sit on a seat and use toilet paper not ferns and leaves. The day just got better.

Moving back along the loch side again I was really taken with the views across the water even though my nemesis was in the back of my mind, in twelve miles I would meet it head on in Drumnadrochit. I reached the village with great trepidation but the village itself was very pretty with touristy shops selling touristy things to, I suppose tourists, of various nationalities. I had a minute for a rest, a snack and a drink and to pull myself together, to paraphrase the quote; I ate and drank for soon I would die not literally, I hoped. I rode off for my High Noon moment, Gary Cooper would have been really proud of me; a man's gotta do…..

I arrived at the turn for the A833 and stopped the bike, my jaw dropped open my worst fears realised, before me stood a sign; 15% for $3/4$ mile. To me that was just shy of 1 in 7 for too long. I needed the dancing feet of Contador more than ever, would I get them or would they be Sergeant's again?

Being a mathematician, well an ex-maths teacher anyway I did a quick calculation and found that $3/4$ mile is 1,207,008 mm and my wheel's circumference is 2198 mm meaning for the hill I would need to turn my wheels approximately 550 times. In my lowest gear one turn of my wheel equals $3/4$ of a revolution of my pedals meaning I had to turn my legs over 411 times before I got to the top, I would count every one.

With a nervous tension cramping my stomach I began the climb, thankfully the rain had abated and it was becoming warm or was that through my efforts? My heart was pumping and my breath was coming in

139

pants, my mouth couldn't open any wider please don't let me swallow a fly. I pushed on my mind wandering to the caterpillar crossing the road before Dalmellington, I'm thinking I must show the same courage and that I would do it for him/her, what am I doing for goodness sake? I read somewhere that the human heart averages 3 billion beats in a lifetime, I think I've used a third of those already when I reached the top and I use the term top very loosely for it is merely a levelling to 10% or 1 in 10 for the next two miles.

At last I reached the real summit and my legs were absolutely shot to pieces for the first time this ride but now after a drink and a few minutes R & R I set off downhill at last. Going down helped of course but my legs were really tired, how do they cycle up the Alps and Pyrenees? I reached *Beau*ly and there was something in the name which made me think it was going to be *Beau*tiful can't think what it was but my impression of it was nothing out of the ordinary, the bit I saw anyway, sorry you Beauly people.

Beyond Beauly it was three miles to dinner at the Ord Arms Hotel in the town of Muir of Ord which seemed to be built around industrial estates. The pub was closed and reflected the dullness of the town itself. You can tell I'm enjoying myself can't you? So we pulled into an area of land outside an Equestrian Centre no less, on the outskirts. The food was the highlight of a very trying morning.

Once again I had a good lunch and filled my belly but all too soon I was ready for the off, would my legs survive? The rain which had held off was now starting to fall again and was forecast to keep falling so I suited up in my rain gear which turned out to be a good decision. I moved off and my legs soon got back into the swing but there were definitely underlining problems with fatigue.

The next village I made my acquaintance with was Conon Bridge which as the name suggests stood astride the river Conon which flowed into the Cromarty Firth. From here it was a short ride to the former county town of the area, Dingwall where I made another mistake. During the map setting up I noticed a cycle route that bypasses the A9, a busy route so I plotted this as an alternative which today I took.

It first took me up an incredibly steep hill between houses, great for my legs, before turning right, still going up but now in some lovely countryside. It was much prettier up here I have to say overlooking the Firth with the fascinating sight of the A9 road bridge stretching a good mile across it. Further on out towards the bay I could also see 'resting oil rigs' must have worked very hard recently a bit like me but resting was merely a dream away for me at the moment.

On the downhill run now and I was going well but unfortunately lost, I needed help which I found from a local lad at a Caravan Park. He put me straight onto the correct road, the B9176 I think, it was hard to tell as my map was disintegrating with the rain. The problem being, I had put myself further along the road than I actually was (obviously not doing as well as I thought).

The road took me to the north of a town called Alness and into what appeared to me, oblivion. It was like a lunar landscape where the human race had forgotten about, the terrain and weather could not have been bleaker. As the mist descended with the rain there was plenty of flora, however the fauna seemed non existent but wait what was that in the grey distance, believe it or not another cyclist. I increased my effort and caught up with him, he had two enormous panniers either side of the back wheel and was travelling not that quickly nor in a straight line. As I approached I could see he had socks on his hands presumably to give him a better grip on the wet handlebars but he did look a sight.

"John O'Groats?" I shouted.

He looked at me and waved one of his socked hands,

"I dunno, I dunno I Spanish."

Could this be Manuel from Fawlty?

I passed him with a hearty "Bon Jour," in true Del Boy fashion and left him with a strange look on his face, to the mercy of the Scottish elements and no doubt dreaming of sunny Espănă.

The rain dropped with gusto as I descended a 12% hill towards the river Averon, which meant of course an uphill on the other side. Going down became quite scary in the increasing rain as my brakes ceased to work efficiently. At the top of the hill on the other side of the river the weather became more like a monsoon, the rain absolutely lashed down with the roads turning into rivers, I was completely wet through. My worries became less of hills and more of crashing on the slippery roads with little or no brakes.

The mist, or was it now cloud had simply enveloped the countryside my only 'view 'was of the wet map and wet tarmac. I wondered about my Spanish friend, I bet he wished he'd stayed in warmer climes. I now got slower and slower and became quite cold the rain had soaked me to the skin, thank heavens there was no Broom Wagon on my tour as I definitely would have been swept up by now. Whilst shuffling through the dreadful weather it brought to mind of many years ago when as a young teacher I played the guitar to accompany my year group in the singing of hymns. One hymn in particular by John Whittler which I enjoyed playing finished with the lines;

"Speak through the earthquake, wind and fire,
O still small voice of calm"

Where was that small voice now in this maelstrom of wind and rain? Later I saw a finger post that brought a wry smile to my face, Strathy 1 mile; unfortunately it was not the Strathy village on the northern coast, which was my stop after tomorrow's stage. Then another sign cheered me a little, a bit like Dartmoor, viewpoint 1 mile. When I arrived, again it was like Dartmoor nothing to see.

At this point, however I started to descend, the hill being fairly steep I tried to go as slowly as I could with my limited brake power. But wait what was that looming from the mist and rain was it a black Mondeo? *O still small voice of calm!* My heart leapt it was of course Mary, what a wonderful sight after travelling through the worst of conditions to see her smiling face. I had a bounce in my pedals as I reached the bottom, she said I had 4 miles to go. After the terrors of the high moor a quote from the seven times consecutive winner of le Tour, Lance Armstrong seemed apposite;

"The pain is so deep and strong that a curtain descends over your brain... Once, someone asked me what pleasure I took in riding for so long. 'Pleasure?' I said. 'I don't understand the question.' I didn't do it for pleasure. I did it for pain."

Not quite the sentiments I felt right now but I understood his meaning in a perverse sort of way if the word pain was replaced by the milder one of satisfaction.

The 4 miles now I was at the bottom proved no problem and I soon cracked them off. I crossed the bridge giving the town its name, a scaled down version of the Sydney Harbour one which spanned the stretch of water between Kyle of Sutherland and the Dornoch Firth and cycled into the town itself. I couldn't help but think of an old Chris de Burgh song which had a line 'An out of season holiday town in the rain' as I passed up the main street to the Dunroamin' Hotel my stop for the night, it seemed to fit it perfectly.

The hotel did not do its web photograph justice, it seemed a little tired, well a lot tired really. Mary told me of a small room with the en-suite in a cupboard but quite frankly I couldn't care all I wanted was a hot shower. The owners of the place were not to be found; we learned later that they were getting their head down whilst they could!

After a reviving shower in the cupboard I felt more like a human being rather than a wet rag and we decided to travel out to see if there was anywhere to eat, not quite fancying the Dunroamin'. However, that was the only bar in town so it was back to the hotel. It had the feel of the type of Scottish bar seen on television in down at heel places, a couple playing pool with a few others scattered around drinking.

There was a sixties downtrodden feel rather than a pleasant pub atmosphere. A foreign couple obviously on holiday simply ignored one another all night, must have been one hell of an argument, or perhaps that's the way they are. One poor chap was sitting at the bar drinking Irn Bru looking at his life over the rim of his glass (with acknowledgements to Ralph McTell's Streets of London) speaking to nobody except the barmaid for more of the Scottish drink.

I was getting quite hungry people watching and having quaffed a couple of beers so we decided to eat and after some deliberation opted for the Chilli. There was a choice of hotness, 1 to 10, I chose 6 being adventurous and Mary chose the 1 not liking spicy hot food. The meals were well presented and surprisingly very good considering the ambience of the place, never judge a book by its cover! I was glad I didn't choose the 10 however, as my meal was fairly hot although the waitress did tell me that somebody asked for a 12, but they *were* Mexican!

After a few more beers, in the words of that great spring Zebedee, it was time for bed, so off we went hoping that tomorrow would bring a better day, it surely could not be worse.

Twenty-four hours after being denied a stage win in Mende, Alexandre Vinokourov (Astana) gained his revenge in Revel, thanks to the kind of late, opportunistic attack that has become his trademark.

Vinokourov's move at the summit of the Côte de Saint-Ferréol - a 1.9km category-three climb that ended 7.5km from the line - was perfectly timed, after Alessandro Ballan (BMC), Nicolas Roche (AG2R) and Damiano Cunego (Lampre) had been among the riders who tried to go clear.

After Vino had fled, Thomas Voeckler (Bbox Bouygues Telecom) chased, with the gap between the pair hovering between eight and ten seconds, and the peloton another five seconds back. As Voeckler cracked, however, and the gap to the leader stretched to thirty seconds, it became clear that the resurgent Vinokourov would claim his first Tour de France stage win since 2007, when he was expelled from the race after testing positive for blood doping.

By strange coincidence, the first of Vinokourov's two stage wins in that Tour - before they were expunged from the record books - also came on stage thirteen, in a time trial in nearby Albi.

Le JO'G Stage 13 2010		Le Tour Stage 13 2010
Fort Augustus – Bonar Bridge		Rodez - Revel
		Winner Vinokourov
Distance	69.842 miles	122.5 miles
Time Cycling	5hr.27m.28s.	4hr.26m.26s.
Average Speed	12.8 mph.	27.59 mph

Stage 14

Tuesday 10th August Bonar Bridge to Strathy

This was a day I did not want to come, the penultimate day of the journey. I had enjoyed myself so much on this ride that I didn't want it to finish, yes even after yesterday!

Of course it hadn't ended yet and it wasn't the last day but then of course there would be the added excitement of finishing with the adrenaline pulsating through my veins. I wondered whether the pro riders on the Tour felt as I did, a little down, I've no doubt the Sports Psychos would have a word for it but a little down would have to do for now, so it is to breakfast, not so much with a heavy heart but certainly with a few pangs of regret.

Breakfast itself was excellent with plenty of good porridge and all the trimmings of a cooked breakfast, just a pity about the room, a bit small with the en-suite in a cupboard, however I slept really well the chilli and beers not causing a problem.

Back to the room to change and out onto the road, the weather was cold with a low mist hanging around the streets hiding the sad look of the town. It was definitely a long sleeve day with the gilet for good measure. I set off along the banks of the Kyle of Sutherland riding the A836 which would keep me company until my lunch stop at an out of the way village called Altnaharra. This is a well known place in winter usually having the coldest night or the most snow in Britain but no problems today. I left the Kyle and headed due north towards the village of Lairg 9 miles away. The roads were empty of traffic but full of the little biting blighters that would swarm over your face if ever you were silly enough to stop to look at the map or take a drink, it was dreadful.

Soon I approached Lairg at the south eastern end of Loch Shin and here it was as though someone had switched on a light, the mist cleared the clouds disappeared and the sun shone brilliantly. The village was quite large because it had been allocated a railway station which I had just passed on my way into the centre.

Beyond Lairg I continued along the banks of the loch until I headed inland and as I looked around I could see the type of scenery I had missed the previous day through the rain. The moonscape of yesterday I could now see was made by the deforestation that had taken place leaving grey branches and tree stumps sticking up here and there, it was an eerie place and very lonely but in its own way quite beautiful.

I kept the river Tirry in my sights as I continued on this 'A' road which had now become a rather rough tarmac single track with passing places, not that these were much in demand as I saw very few cars, about four every hour! I came to a sign at the side of the road that simply said Crask. I looked at the map but could find no village marked, however having reached the top of a hill it was set out before me, the thriving metropolis of one house and one pub/hotel, I could imagine the raves on a Saturday night.

From Lairg I had been travelling upwards from 278 feet above sea level to the Crask hill at 866 feet above sea level gently with some fantastic wild scenery. I tore myself away from the 'busy' village of Crask and continued now with the river Vagastie as my guide through what I can only describe as one of the most scenic valleys I have ever seen. A lonely place bordered with fantastic hills and mountains, the road having been recently resurfaced, some cycle ride this.

All the training back home in the wind and the rain and the desperate cycle ride of yesterday was all worth the trouble just to be here in the Strath Vagastie region alone with the sun on my back and only these damn midges for company! As I rode out of the valley over the hill I spotted Mary with her camera flagging me down for lunch. She informed me that the Altnaharra hotel was closed and the midges were an absolute nightmare in the village, better to eat here in the car with the view down the valley. No sooner had I stopped when a swarm of the blighters attacked my face I couldn't wait to jump in the car and safety.

The car was more like a sauna with all the doors and windows closed in an attempt to keep from being bitten to death whilst lunch was prepared and then eaten with gusto. Mary regaled me of her experience in trying to buy a newspaper in the village. She asked a local workman who said,
"If you go that way you have got 25 miles to go, if you go that way you have 30 miles to go and if you walk over the hills you have 13 miles to go; lady you don't get a newspaper here!"

It was very pleasant eating my food looking down the valley with the sun glinting off the river I could quite easily have closed my eyes and drifted away in the warmth. I'm sure the riders in the Tour would have definitely been jealous when you see them eating on the 'hoof' never stopping to rest. Well my time came to cut short my stay and I was off to Strathy on the northern coast, a tingle of excitement hit me, the NORTHERN coast! Nearly there.

I cycled from our vantage point down into Altnaharra and I concurred with Mary, good decision to eat on the hill top. It was hot and windless with the ubiquitous gnat on the wing. I left the A836 after the village turning right which took me along the shores of Loch Naver on the B873 an even smaller road which twisted and turned went up and down but never failed to excite with its loneliness and great views of the loch with the mountains as a backdrop.

Another great advantage of this road that now I was travellng east and the wind was coming from the west, you work it out as to why there was a smile on my face. Eventually at the end of the loch I turned northwards following yet another river, the Naver which flowed from the loch to the sea into Torrisdale Bay on the NORTHERN coast!

Through the Naver Forest I went, marvelling at the beauty of the place. I've always been an admirer of high fells with lonely windswept grasslands and heathers so this stage has been a wonder to behold. It was an experience to cycle the banks of rivers with the constant burbling and gurgling of the water to keep you company the afternoon just slid by.

It was sheer magic to be on a bike in the peace and quiet but somehow I had joined the B871 so I noted on a signpost in the little hamlet of Chealamy so I stopped to check my map. A car appeared in front of me from apparently nowhere and screeched to a halt in a skid and a cloud of dust. The window wound down and a voice called out,

"Ye lost?"

"No I'm fine," I replied, and with a smile he screeched off again, then peace and quiet descended once more, it is amazing how thoughtful people can be. Looking at the map I noticed that I was only about 8 miles or so from the coast at Bettyhill. The landlady of the Dunroamin' sucked in her cheeks at the thought of me travelling the route to Bettyhill,

"What with the long hill up to Bettyhill and the alpine bends you'll do well today," she bemoaned.

Thanks for that, I thought.

Well I'm here now so Bettyhill here I come. I came back onto the A836 which would take me to John O'Groats but first I needed to get to Strathy. I crossed the river as it poured into the estuary and said my final goodbye as I approached the hill to the village at the top, I spied my first sign for John O'Groats, 55 miles to go I pedalled with a spring in my step. It was a long and protracted slope but good views kept my mind off the pain. Near the top there was a sign by the side of the road;

"Shop next turn right open 8 days a week"

It reminded me of an old Beatles song, strange how my mind always seemed to wander when I climbed the hills must be the exhaustion.

On and on I went until finally I reached the top, the view of the beach looked great, Farr Bay, it was wild and rugged with the wind blowing off the sea. Of course at the top of the hill one must go down and looking further on the dreaded alpine bends I heard about previously. Off I go Wheeeeeeeeee down the hill and Oooooooooooh round the bends! The road meandered side to side beyond the alpines but also up and down, however the little traffic helped to keep me in high spirits. This was another roller coaster of a ride but felt more like Alton towers at times!

I passed my back up driver on the road later who informed me that I have only another mile to go before I reached the Strathy Inn, none too soon either for it had been a beautiful but over the last few miles a very tiring day. When I asked Mary about the accommodation, good or bad considering the en-suite cupboard, thankfully she replied in the most positive of terms. I soon arrived at the Strathy Inn and dispatched my bike in the garage for the night, I went into the hotel and was offered, as in the Old Manse, tea and biscuits how very civilised.

After the drink we decided to go for a little spin in the car to while away the time before our evening meal. It was a lovely area with fabulous views down to the sea all along the coast. We visited the local cemetery, not because I thought I might end up there later I hasten to add, but simply because it looked so beautiful on the hill and as always a great view. Back to the pub for a wonderful meal of Moroccan lamb tagine and a couple of beers, unbelievably Boddingtons from Manchester being one!

Now remember me telling you about the conversation with the man on the ferry about the good Dr. Geebers, the homeless man from Skelmersdale; well who should walk into the pub, but the very same. He told us that he was originally from Northern Ireland but made homeless in Brighton, from whence he started his journey. We had a good chat with him and he explained he was making his way to John O'Groats similar to us but by foot and then moving down the east coast back to Brighton.

After the journey he was going to write a book about his travels with the money going for the plight of the homeless. He was certainly full of the Irish blarney and the gift of the gab although it didn't all quite ring true the things he said and the landlord wasn't that impressed either. Pretty soon I was getting tired, so Mary and I returned to our room leaving the landlord to deal with the walking Dr. Geebers.

He did, I am pleased to say, make John O'Groats on the 20th August nine days after me, apparently he made a sculpture which was of a boat made from the local rocks and pebbles.

Mark Cavendish of HTC-Columbia put his stamp on the sprint finishes of this year's Tour, with his fourth mass sprint victory in Bordeaux looking easier than ever. He had a five-bike length gap over Julian Dean (Garmin-Transitions) and Alessandro Petacchi (Lampre-Farnese Vini).

In the battle for the green jersey, Petacchi had the upper hand. His third place finish gave him enough points to snatch it off the shoulders of Thor Hushovd (Cervelo TestTeam), who went too early in the wind and finished a disappointing 13th.

"I only want to win, not matter by how much," Cavendish said. "When Petacchi went, I thought, that's it. But then it was pretty easy."

It was Cavendish's 14th career Tour stage win, all gathered within only three years. He has now outdistanced his mentor Erik Zabel, who himself won in Bordeaux in 1995 and 1997. "I have never seen anyone like Mark," said the old master, who gave his protégé several hugs after the stage.

Le JO'G Stage 14 2010		Le Tour Stage 18 2010
Bonar Bridge - Strathy		Salies-de-Bearn –
		Bordeaux
	Winner	Cavendish
Distance	69.842 miles	123.75 miles
Time Cycling	5hr.27m.28s.	4hr.37m.09s.
Average Speed	12.8 mph.	26.79 mph

Stage 15

Wednesday 11th August Strathy to John O'Groats

I awoke on the last day not knowing whether to be happy or sad, happy to have made the last day but sad that it was all coming to an end, was it really fifteen days ago since I started. This wasn't just the ride coming to the end but all the twelve months of planning coming to fruition, all finished.

I got out of the bed a little stiff in the old joints but happy for one last push to the finish. I drew back the curtains in the hope of good weather continuing from yesterday but looked at the horizontal rain, disappointment filled my heart for I wanted to wear all my best gear for the finale and waterproofs just didn't hack it. When I then realised the rain was horizontal because the wind was from the north and east disappointment turned to desperation, thankfully it was only 40 odd miles to the finish.

Down to breakfast or should I say through the door for breakfast, as we ate just in the next room on the nearest table to our door, could they hear my creaking joints? A good breakfast it was, thick porridge and excellent poached eggs on toast to see me on my way. I once read in a book that the definition of insanity is doing the same things over and over again but expecting different outcomes. It seemed I had been doing that for 14 days expecting different outcomes but all I got was the same euphoria and tiredness each and every night, does that make me mad? Your guess is as good as mine, anyway here's another mad day with the inevitable finish but this time at John O'Groats.

The rain had eased and by 9.20 I set off, a little late but as it was a fairly shortish journey today who was counting. I hit the road running with a great downhill stretch followed by a not so great uphill stretch. This seemed to be the norm for the first part of the ride.

I came across another Reynard dead but not buried at the side of the road another fox free night for the bunny population. I got to thinking that these road kills were a bit like Orkney buses, you don't see one for ages then two come round in eight days! I suppose across the Channel on the other ride, their road kill would consist of snails and frogs something they would probably take home and eat!

Anyway back to my ride, I was now passing through Strathy village with signs for East and West Strathy strangely pointing north and south? The landlord of the Inn informed me this morning that the first ten miles are a bit up and down; he was not wrong but after that it simply became undulating. I was inclined to remember the great proverb; one man's undulations are another man's hills or something like that.

The next village on the lonely road was Melvich which had me going inland to come back out again but this time uphill in the face of the wind. I could not seem to believe I was on the last 3 maps of the book, butterflies in my tummy were once again setting off and if the chaos theory was to be believed they would cause mayhem somewhere else in the world.

The road was very open with windswept grasslands surrounding me as I made my quiet way east. I noticed a house to my left that was virtually on the cliff edge and beyond that house I could see only sea, the next house in that direction would be in Iceland, looking I supposed a lot different in style. Crazy what goes through your mind, when in the distance I fancied I could see Moon Base Alpha was I now hallucinating? The answer was of course not, it all became clear when I met the village of Reay situated close to the power station of Dounreay, funnily enough with 6 wind turbines just behind, could that be the past and the future or should it be the future and the past?

From here the road was incredibly straight proving that not only the Romans could build straight roads but a bit boring for this cyclist just looking straight ahead at the same view, still it was good from side to side though. A turn to the right saw me riding into the small village of Bridge of Forss then a couple of miles gradually up and then a couple down I rode into the large town of Thurso whose name was derived from old Norse for Bull's Water, are they taking the p---?

The Vikings who lived around here also took a leaf out of the Roman book of roads for beyond here 4 miles of straight black tarmac loomed ahead, that's something to look forward to. Will Smith was born in Thurso, I bet that was a surprise to you. Oh not that Will Smith of Men in Black fame and other films but William Alexander Smith of founding the Boy's Brigade type of fame, amazing what you learn riding a bike.

Through the town but not before a toilet stop, is that too much information? I crossed the bridge over the river Thurso and continued on the 4 mile straight to the village of Castletown. This was full of dark granite buildings giving an appearance of despair but I'm sure most of the people were just happy to live there, perhaps the buildings just needed a clean.

After leaving the village I embarked on the hardest bit of the stage so far. It took me around Dunnet Bay, a part of the ride which should have been enjoyable but with the wind in my face blowing off the sea I found it less so. Two and a half miles of cold northerly wind was it really the height of summer? But at least the sun was now shining.

Soldiering on and the road turned eastwards I came across a left turning for Dunnet Head, the most northerly point on mainland Britain. Philosophically I suppose, I should have made a detour to cycle to the most northerly point, however 5 miles there and 5 miles back threw philosophy out of the window but wasn't that what this ride should have been about? However, having endured the trip around the bay my legs were a bit weary with more energy perhaps so, but not today.

I continued on to Mey a little village that has the Queen Mother's Castle and also the Castle Arms pub my so called stop for lunch and my bed for the night. So called because I realised along the way that I had miscounted the mileage, there should have been 17 miles to go at this point but fortunately for me it was only 7. As it was not worth stopping for lunch my better half and I decided that to continue to John O'Groats would be the better option and have something to eat afterwards.

With the knowledge of only seven more miles to the finish I set off with a new lease of life Dunnet Bay long forgotten. Pretty soon I turned the maps over in my wallet to find that I was on the last one,

"THE LAST ONE" I shouted to no-one in particular with about 3 miles to go. I was averaging a decent speed, not quite the HTC Columbia team standard dragging Mark Cavendish to the line but over 14mph and I wanted to keep that up so I didn't slow down until closer to the end.

Simon my son had told me to soak up the finish, take it all in look around. This I did, imagining the crowds, the adulation, the cheering, what a feeling, wonderful absolutely wonderful. I began to savour the moment and with the sun shining on me what more could I wish for? The Champs Elysee on a final Sunday of course!

The old A836 had been a good companion to me since Bonar Bridge and apart from the Naver valley (A871) it had seen me through 'til the end, well almost. The final half mile took me on the A99 to the signpost itself. I turned left onto this road and fortunately it was slightly downhill, I coasted home wind or no wind.

There are no tired legs on the Champs – Elysees or so they say, although the Irish cyclist Paul Kimmage a one time domestique and a writer of a book about his experiences on the Tour and drugs, dispels the charm of that by adding no random dope samples are taken on the last stage. My legs were certainly not tired but thank heavens for the lack of drug testing I'm sure my pain killers would not be missed!

I saw the gathering of buildings coming closer and my body started to tingle with excitement. It was now I remembered back to my youth how bad I was at riding without hands, would I fall at the last hurdle, how embarrassing would that be, could you imagine any of the pro riders in Le Tour doing that?

I tentatively let go of the bars and managed to get my arms to 45 degrees arthritic shoulders notwithstanding. Of course I wanted to ride in to the sound of Nimrod on my MP3 player which I now couldn't do but to compensate I must have looked like a Harrier Jump Jet on a vertical take off (cue back cover). I did manage the short distance and fell into the arms of Mary before taking in the final hundred yards or so to the signpost itself.

At the post everything became surreal, I was treated to an ovation from the crowd of sightseers gathered around, well at least five people anyway. Two young teenage lads from Ealing in London had just finished and were having their photograph taken so I had to wait my turn.

Mary, unbeknown to me had painted a pint mug, bought a T-shirt, card and a bottle of champagne which she awarded me at the finish. When the 'crowd' saw this they went 'ecstatic' taking photographs shaking me by the hand, I felt really sorry for the two London boys.

What a beautiful moment my outside caterer conjured up, I had tears in my eyes and again now writing about it. It will live with me forever. What a time, what an achievement for us both on a wonderful day. A dream came true helped by my most patient wife. As the French writer Guy de Maupassant once said, "What's the point of triumph if you cannot share it with someone?"

After the photo session I loaded up the car with my bike for the last time and then it was back to the Castle Arms to get changed. A visit to a local café for lunch then a trip to Castle Mey followed by Dunnet Head (much easier by car) saw me back at the pub to finish off the champers. Another excellent meal in the dining room and a few beers in the bar with the company of some local youngsters and a couple from the Midlands, visiting the lady's mum in a nursing home. Soon my eyes began to close the trials of the day had caught up with me and tonight I was sure I was going to sleep well.

After the biggest fight in his cycling life, Alberto Contador has won a third Tour de France.

"This victory cost me a lot," he said, "and I'm very moved. I suffered a lot, but that's what you have to do to win the Tour."

When the fat lady was warming up her vocal cords, readying her wide-berthed-self to sing to the tune of the Spanish national anthem, with all his might and power, down came HTC-Columbia's Mark Cavendish on the Champs-Élysées, proving for a fifth time this race, he still is the world's best sprinter.

"Bernie took me to the tunnel the last time and Tony did a really good job to drop me on the wheel of Petacchi in the last kilometer" said the 25-year-old, who holds a future as bright as the star of Sirius, "We came out of that last corner and I just jumped... Every sprint in the Tour you try and save as much energy as possible, but the Champs-Élysées, you've got nothing to save your energy for - you just go balls-out to the line, and that's kind of what I did today."

Perhaps the best story of this Tour is the legacy it leaves. Three weeks ago on July 3, so many automatically assumed a Contador victory was a done deal. Few thought 27-year-old 'Pistolero' would come so close to defeat at the hands of a boyish-faced, slightly naïve Luxembourger 18 months his junior - the man we know as Andy Schleck of Team Saxo Bank.

Unfortunately for the maillot jaune *and* Le Tour *Alberto Contador was found guilty of using the banned drug clenbuterol and is facing a one year suspension pending appeals.*

Le JO'G Stage 15 2010		Le Tour Stage 20 2010
Strathy – John O'Groats		Longjumeau - Paris
		Winner Cavendish
Distance	42.361miles	64.063miles
Time Cycling	2hr.57m.59s.	2hr.42m.21s.
Average Speed	14.3 mph.	23.68 mph

No more Stages

Thursday 12th August Mey – Home

This was of course the journey home by car and I got to use the Sat Nav instead of maps! Mary told me it had been playing up with the sound disappearing let's hope we make it back before laryngitis steps in.

Firstly breakfast, all the trimmings now, a full Scottish with everything you can think of and a bit more. During the meal we chatted with the landlord about the Queen Mother and the Castle of Mey just up the road. He told us of a visit she made to the pub for some painting she was to receive from a local artist, he had a photograph and would show it to us before we left for home.

After breakfast the landlord took us into the room where we had dinner the previous night. He asked Mary to stand behind a chair whilst he explained about the photograph on the wall. He talked about the fireplace in the photo similar to the one on our left, the table similar to the one in front, the window similar to the one next to the fire then suddenly he said,
"You're standing in exactly the same place as the Queen Mother!" What a brilliant raconteur and didn't he enjoy doing it. We had a good laugh but all too soon it was time to leave.

The Sat Nav was showing the way to Thurso then after down the A9 to the east coast. Interestingly enough I refused to go on the A9 on my trip up because of fear of too much traffic, it was just the opposite but certainly not as picturesque as the western side. If I thought I had made the incorrect decision about coming up on the A9 I was proved wrong when I saw poor cyclists approaching some horrendous hills north of Helmsdale on the coast with the wind blowing strongly into their faces.

We followed the A9 through Brora and over Cromaty Firth to other places south eventually skirting in between Glasgow and Edinburgh then finally down the M6, home at last after about 10 hours hard driving, what an amazing distance.

Epilogue

All good bike races have a Prologue, mine also has an Epilogue, but what can I say in this, some great philosophical comments, some sayings worthy of note? Well perhaps not but I'll give it a go.

Firstly the statistics of the ride:

Total mileage clocked by my cycle odometer	984.272
Average mph for whole journey	13.85
Average calorie consumption per day	2110

Secondly what lessons have I learned in this great journey of ours?

I think I can say without doubt, do not take anyone or anything for granted. Mary performed admirably throughout the journey keeping me going with food and a happy smiling face at all times, I've said it before but this could not have been done without her great backup. Don't take small hills for granted for they can come back and bite you, tiring your legs constantly.

To be mentally tough, I thought the amount of time I had spent cycling on my own would mean doing this alone would be no problem. However, from Muir of Ord over to Bonar Bridge adverse weather conditions proved extremely difficult, the worst I have ever faced, oh for a companion then to share the journey and the pain.

Never pass a toilet. The number of times I had to go for a pee was innumerable doing it on the bike was not an option.

Don't change up too soon after coming to the top of a hill, you will lose what little momentum you have.

Keep focused whilst on the hill do not lose concentration or before you know where you are your cadence is slowing and once again momentum is getting lost. I remembered watching Le Tour on Eurosport when David Harmon asked a co-commentator, a female cyclist I missed her name, the best way to climb the mountains on the Grand Tours. She said that one of the past greats (missed his name too) reckoned you should caress the mountain, whatever that meant!

I think you should try to be at one with the hill and try to keep a rhythm if at all possible, that probably doesn't sound much better either, however, we are talking of longer hills not sharp 1 in 4s etc. then you just give it all you've got and hope for the best!

Hills in the distance are never as bad as they look, well perhaps sometimes they are!

I hope this book has been of some use to future end to enders and not just trying to teach grandmas to suck eggs and that it gives some idea of my route with its difficulties and of course its countless rewards with wonderful scenery and great satisfaction.

Finally what did we get out of this journey......As the saying goes...... Go for it and enjoy the ride.
We most certainly did!

Acknowledgements

Firstly; the CTC organization for providing me with an excellent route.

Secondly: the Anquet Website for supplying me with superb maps and allowing me the ability to draw the route electronically.

Thirdly: it has to be Wikipedia. When I set out the route I checked all the towns and villages I would be passing through on the website for interesting titbits. I cannot, of course guarantee the correctness of the information used but it was interesting anyway.

Fourthly: Tim Moore the writer of 'French Revolutions' an immensely funny read which gave me the confidence to write my own story.

Fifthly: The Cycling News website for giving me the information concerning the winning of the stages in the Tour de France 2010

In the old cliché last but certainly not least my family, Mary with her patience, for giving me the help and assistance in doing the journey and the push for me to write my book and my dad who listened with great enthusiasm to all my tales of woe and happiness after each day on the telephone.

5353227R00094

Printed in Great Britain
by Amazon.co.uk, Ltd.,
Marston Gate.